A Sound Start

the schools' instrumental music service

WITHDRAWN FROM
THE LIBRARY

UNIVERSITY OF

D0488843

A Sound Start
the schools' instrumental music service

Shirley Cleave
and
Karen Dust

NFER-NELSON

Published by The NFER-NELSON Publishing Company Ltd.,
Darville House, 2 Oxford Road East,
Windsor, Berkshire SL4 1DF, England

First Published 1989
© 1989, National Foundation for Educational Research

British Library Cataloguing in Publication Data
   Cleave, Shirley
      A Sound Start: the schools' instumental
      music service.
      1. Schools. Curriculum subjects: Music
      I. Title II. Dust, Karen.
      780'.71

         ISBN 0-7005-0871-6
         ISBN 0-7005-0872-4 Pbk

All rights reserved, including translation.
No part of this publication may be reproduced
or transmitted in any form or by any means,
electronic or mechanical, including photocopying,
recording or duplication in any information
storage and retrieval system, without permission
in writing from the publishers.

Typeset by First Page Ltd., Watford.
Printed by Billing & Sons Ltd, Worcester

ISBN 0 7005 0871 6 (Hardback)
Code 8305 02 1

ISBN 0 7005 0872 4 (Paperback)
Code 8306 02 1

KING ALFRED'S COLLEGE
WINCHESTER

375.78   97221
CLE

Contents

List of Tables

The National Foundation for Educational Research

The National Foundation for Educational Research in England and Wales was founded in 1946 and is Britain's leading educational research institution. It is an independent body undertaking research and development projects on issues of current interest in all sectors of the public educational system. Its membership includes all the local education authorities in England and Wales, the main teachers' associations, and a large number of other major organizations with educational interests.

Its approach is scientific, apolitical and non-partisan. By means of research projects and extensive field surveys it has provided objective evidence on important educational issues for the use of teachers, administrators, parents and the research community. The expert and experienced staff that has been built up over the years enables the Foundation to make use of a wide range of modern research techniques, and, in addition to its own work, it undertakes a large number of specially sponsored projects at the request of government departments and other agencies.

The major part of the research programme relates to the maintained educational sector – primary, secondary and further education. A further significant element has to do specifically with local education authorities and training institutions. The current programme includes work on the education of pupils with special needs, monitoring of pupil performance, staff development, national evaluation and major curriculum programmes, test development, and information technology in schools. The Foundation is also the national agency for a number of international research and information exchange networks.

The NFER-NELSON Publishing Company are the main publishers of the Foundation's research reports. These reports are now available in the *NFER Research Library*, a collection which provides the educational community with up-to-date research into a wide variety of subject areas. In addition, the Foundation and NFER-NELSON work closely together to provide a wide range of open and closed educational tests and a test advisory service. NFER-NELSON also publish *Educational Research*, the termly journal of the Foundation.

Acknowledgements

We welcome the opportunity to thank the many people who have contributed to the success of this NFER-funded project. We wish to thank the advisers and heads of service who completed our questionnaire, and all those who gave so much of their time to speak with us and show us how the service operated in their authority. Special thanks go to the instrumental teachers who allowed us to accompany them on their visits to schools and observe them at work. We are grateful also to HMSO for granting permission for the reproduction of an extract from the *School Teachers' Pay and Conditions Document 1987.*

We would like to extend a special word of thanks to Muriel Blackwell (Music Adviser, Brent), Helena Braithwaite (Music Adviser, South Glamorgan), Edmond Fivet (Director, Junior Department of the Royal College of Music), Richard Hallam (Assistant County Music Adviser, Oxfordshire), Anthony Howie (Head of Creative Arts and PE Faculty, Holland Park School) and Gillian Wills (formerly of the SCDC *Arts in Schools* project) for their support, help and advice throughout the research.

We are grateful to our colleagues at the NFER. In particular, we would like to thank Seamus Hegarty for his initial encouragement in establishing the project, and Judy Bradley who took over the directorship of the project; Felicity Fletcher-Campbell and David Sims for their constructive comments on the final draft of the report; Deborah Billings for her excellent secretarial skills and the many hours spent preparing the manuscript; and Mary Hargreaves and Shani Wright for their design of the diagrams in this report.

1 Introduction

This book reports the findings from a research study of the instrumental music service provided by local education authorities for children of school age. The study was sponsored and carried out by the National Foundation for Educational Research from January 1986 to September 1987, and formed part of the Foundation's developing programme of research in the expressive arts. The purpose of the study was to describe LEA instrumental music provision in England and Wales, and to examine its contribution to the music education of primary and secondary pupils. This was the first major study of the instrumental music service to be conducted on a national scale.

Virtually all LEAs employ a team of peripatetic instrumental teachers to work in schools, colleges and music centres. A wide range of instruments is covered: strings, woodwind, brass and percussion are taught in almost all authorities, and some LEAs also offer tuition in guitar, keyboards, ethnic and early instruments and voice. Instrumental teachers visit most secondary and middle schools and some primary schools. Some selection inevitably occurs with regard to which pupils receive tuition. Lessons take place mainly in school, but most authorities also promote a variety of musical activities outside normal school hours in schools or other premises designated as music centres. Activities may include advanced or specialist tuition not otherwise available in schools, aural and musicianship classes, and various forms of ensemble including orchestras, bands and choirs.

The research was timely: recent trends in education, coupled with continuing economic constraints, were causing many local authorities to review their service. In 1984, an inquiry conducted by Her Majesty's Inspectorate of Schools (HMI) revealed significant regional variations in policy and provision, and while some authorities had increased their instrumental staff and improved their service, others had made substantial reductions and, in one case, suspended the service entirely for several years. However, most Chief Education Officers considered instrumental music to be 'an integral part of the curriculum' and, despite restrictions imposed by diminishing resources, the service provided by LEAs continued to play an important role in music education.

In this climate of change and re-appraisal, the NFER study was generally welcomed as a means of providing information which would assist authorities and schools in reviewing existing services and planning for the future. To obtain this information the research was divided into three parts: an initial exploratory stage, a selection of in-depth case studies and, finally, a national survey.

During the exploratory stage, the research team contacted a range of people involved in instrumental music tuition. Discussions were held with advisers, heads of service and school staff in a variety of authorities across the country, and with tutors in music colleges and teacher training institutions. Contacts were also established with national and international music associations and organizations. The information gathered at this stage enabled the team to identify the key issues to be explored in the case studies and survey.

For the second stage of the research, the team selected four very different LEAs in which to make an in-depth study of the instrumental music service in action. The LEAs were situated in northern, southern, central and eastern England. Two were counties with a mixture of rural and urban areas; two were metropolitan districts. Populations ranged in size from 250,000 in the smallest case study to 1,500,000 in the largest, and local councils were of various political persuasions.

The case studies enabled the research team to examine how the service operated in each area. The team also wanted to explore the relationship between instrumental teachers and their schools and to look at liaison between all parties involved at every level of the instrumental service. Interviews were held with advisers, instrumental teachers, school-based staff, parents and pupils. Instrumental lessons were observed in a selection of schools representing primary, secondary and middle school systems and including grammar and comprehensive schools. The team also spent time with instrumental staff in music centres and attended rehearsals and performances. Visits to case-study LEAs took place in the summer and autumn terms; this enabled the team to observe pupils who were about to leave school, those who were taking up instrumental tuition for the first time and those who were transferring from the primary to secondary sector. Altogether, more than 100 interviews and 100 observations of lessons and other musical activities were carried out at this stage.

Issues illuminated by the case-study work formed the basis of the national survey. A questionnaire exploring these issues was sent to music advisers in all LEAs in England and Wales including the island authorities of Jersey, Guernsey, Scilly and Man. The questionnaire sought information on the history and perceived purpose of the instrumental music service, organization and administration, staffing and resources, the provision and maintenance of instruments, the selection of schools and pupils to receive tuition, the recording of pupil progress, arrangements for children with special needs and exceptional talent, opportunities for ensemble work, and innovations and plans for change. (Copies of the questionnaire are obtainable from the NFER Library, The Mere, Upton Park, Slough.)

Ninety-four (87 per cent) of the 108 LEAs completed the questionnaire. Of the remainder, one had no instrumental music service at the time (preparations were being made to set it up again), two were unable to take part for various reasons and 11 did not respond. The distribution of LEAs participating in the survey is shown in Table 1.1.

Table 1.1:   *LEAs participating in the survey*

LEAs	(n)	Taking part in survey
English counties	(39)	36
Metropolitan districts	(36)	29
London boroughs	(21)	17
Islands	(4)	4
Wales	(8)	8
	(108)	94

Although the questionnaire was sent in the first instance to the music adviser, not all LEAs had an adviser for music and in these cases the questionnaire was completed by the person responsible for running the instrumental music service or, in one case, the assistant director of education. Some advisers passed the questionnaire on to their heads of service or completed it jointly with them. The distribution of questionnaire respondents is shown in Table 1.2.

Table 1.2:   *Respondents completing the questionnaire (94 LEAs)*

Respondents	LEAs
Music adviser	63
Head of instrumental service	27
Music adviser jointly with head of service	3
Assistant director of education	1
	94

The information gathered from the three stages of the research is drawn together in the following chapters. Chapter 2, pp. 5–7, describes the historical background and development of the instrumental music service, and considers the perceived purpose and role of the service in relation to recent trends and changes in education. Chapter 3, pp. 18–40, describes the staffing and management of the service and Chapter 4, pp. 41–54, gives details on instruments and financial resources. Attention is then focused on the 'consumers' of the service. Chapter 5, pp. 55–84, describes the level of provision in terms of the schools and children selected for instrumental tuition, and discusses ways of maximizing continuity and monitoring progress. Chapter 6, pp. 85–107, is concerned with the instrumental service in the school and Chapter 7, pp. 108–141, with the service in the music centre*. The book concludes with Chapter 8 which summarizes the main issues, raises questions for those re-appraising their service and offers a number of recommendations for urgent consideration.

---

* The term 'music centre' is used throughout this book to include centres which in some LEAs are designated music 'schools' but which in most respects function as music centres.

2 Historical and Recent Contexts

This chapter sets the scene by first outlining the development of LEA instrumental music services and then describing their current context. Reference is made to recent trends and changes in education, and the chapter concludes with a discussion of the perceived purposes of an instrumental service and some of the local factors which affect its implementation.

Origins and development of LEA instrumental music services

The beginnings of the instrumental music service are obscure. There is no single date on which the service was established in England and Wales. Instead, the development of instrumental music in schools can be attributed to a variety of sources and influences in different parts of the country.

Asked when an instrumental music service was established in their authority, some respondents were able to trace its origins back to the years before the Second World War. Others, particularly in the more recently created metropolitan districts, dated their service from the organization of their LEA into its present form. Details of the establishment of instrumental music services in the 94 LEAs responding to our survey are given in Table 2.1.

The 1940s and before

Eleven LEAs reported the beginnings of an instrumental music service in the 1940s or earlier. Some of these paid tribute to the enterprising

Table 2.1: *Approximate dates when LEA instrumental music services were established (94 LEAs)*

Date	English counties	Metropolitan districts	London boroughs	Islands	Wales	No. LEAs	% LEAs
1940s and earlier	8	1	1	0	1	11	12
1950s	8	0	0	0	3	11	12
1960s	11	13	12	1	1	38	40
1970s	3	13	3	3	1	23	24
1980s	0	1	1	0	0	2	2
Not known	6	1	0	0	2	9	10
	36	29	17	4	8	94	100

Although Metropolitan districts were not created in their present form until the early seventies, instrumental music schemes already existed in some of the towns and boroughs in these areas. The same is true for several of the other LEAs which came into being with the formation of the London boroughs in the sixties and local authority reorganization in 1974.

efforts of enthusiastic individuals who had begun by teaching school-children in their locality to play an instrument. One such example was Arthur Allsop, a market gardener from Selby, who could play the violin particularly well. He was invited by a headteacher to give lessons after school and his work led eventually to the formation of the Doncaster Schools' Orchestra. Others, especially in the counties, were able to trace the roots of their service back to the Rural Music School movement which began in 1929 with the foundation of the Hert-fordshire Rural Music School at Hitchin.

According to Trodd (1978), group instrumental tuition in elementary schools began soon after the First World War when a largely commercial venture made violin playing accessible to young children through a series of graded melodies known as the Maidstone system. Group violin tuition was further advanced by John Hullah Brown who devised a simply constructed violin which he called the 'violinda', and his courses for teachers helped to bring instrumental tuition within the reach of large groups of young pupils during the 1930s and 1940s.

During this period, instrumental tuition was taking root in other ways. For example, Taylor (1979) describes the use of percussion instruments such as drums, tambourines, triangles and cymbals from as early as 1909, and notes that percussion band, violin and wind classes were encouraged by the non-competitive festival movement founded by Ulric Brunner in 1927. These festivals provided a strong impetus to instrumental work in schools and in particular to the formation of school orchestras. Awareness of instrumental tuition was no doubt raised among teachers generally by the first large-scale Schools' Music Festival which was staged by the newly-founded Schools Music Association in the Royal Albert Hall in 1939.

The post-war years of the 1940s saw a number of major events in music education. The National Youth Orchestra of Wales was formed in 1945 and was followed two years later by the National Youth Orchestra of Great Britain. Instrumental lessons, particularly in violin, were gradually becoming more widespread in schools and in 1947 the Ministry of Education mounted its first short course for teachers of strings. In the same year the Music Advisers National Association was established.

The 1950s

Music advisers were increasingly being appointed by LEAs to develop musical activities in schools, and by the end of the 1950s almost half the authorities in the country had a music adviser (Taylor, *ibid.*). Some of them recruited peripatetic staff and set up instrumental teaching schemes which provided the basis for their instrumental service today: 11 of the counties in our survey (eight in England and three in Wales) owed the beginnings of their service to this period.

With the development of instrumental schemes came an upsurge in LEA Saturday music centres and a proliferation of youth bands and orchestras. The National Schools Brass Band Association was founded in 1952, and in the same year the National Youth Brass Band was established, to be followed two years later by the British Youth Symphony Orchestra. The recorder was also becoming increasingly popular as an instrument which could be taught in schools. This owed much to the work of Carl Dolmetsch and his team who had revived interest in early musical instruments. Recorders also had the advantage of being relatively cheap and easy to produce. The recorder was therefore accessible to large numbers of children and offered further possibilities when combined with percussion, strings or voices.

The 1960s and 1970s

During the 1960s and 1970s, instrumental teaching flourished and developed, and by the end of this period the majority of LEAs had established an instrumental service (see Table 2.1). As more children learned to play musical instruments, the need for opportunities to perform together increased and in 1961 the National Association of Youth Orchestras was formed in order to represent and foster the development of youth and inter-school orchestras throughout the country. The creation of the London boroughs in the 1960s, and the advent of the metropolitan districts and reorganization of boundaries in the 1970s, resulted in the formation of many new LEAs with the opportunity either to set up instrumental services or to take over those which already existed in their area. Provision was expanding with regard to both the range of instruments taught and the kind of music played, and was reflected in the establishment of orchestras such as the National Youth Jazz in 1965 and the British Youth Wind in 1968. Meanwhile, the Ministry of Education (soon to become the Department of Education and Science) broadened its short courses for teachers to include wind, brass, orchestral and symphonic ensemble experience. During the same period a number of specialist schools, such as the Purcell and Yehudi Menuhin schools, were opened for children of exceptional musical ability, and other long-established schools with a choral tradition, such as Chetham's Hospital and Wells Cathedral School, became co-educational and dramatically increased their provision for instrumentally talented pupils.

At the start of the 1970s, group violin tuition received another boost when children trained by the Suzuki method toured England. Shinichi Suzuki had developed a teaching method by which thousands of very young Japanese children had learned to play the violin on instruments scaled down to sizes from a half to a sixteenth. The method subsequently spread westwards where it attracted considerable interest, and a research programme into its adaptation was undertaken by the Rural Music Schools Association which has since done much to further its use in this country.

The festival movement continued to grow in popularity, and in 1971 the first National Festival of Music for Youth, with its emphasis on group rather than solo performances, was held. This was followed in 1975 by the first Schools Prom. LEA music centre provision was increasing and by 1977 an inquiry into the training of musicians (Calouste Gulbenkian Foundation, 1978) revealed that almost all authorities had music centres.

Local government reorganization

In many LEAs the reorganization of local authority boundaries in 1974 was to have an effect on the instrumental music service which is still felt today. Services in the metropolitan districts and counties were most affected by the changes; least affected were the London boroughs and island authorities. Altogether, instrumental music services in two-thirds of the LEAs in our survey were affected by the reorganization (Table 2.2).

Table 2.2: *Instrumental music services affected by 1974 local government reorganization (94 LEAs)*

Whether affected	English counties	Metropolitan districts	London boroughs	Islands	Wales	No. LEAs	% LEAs
Affected	27	26	2	0	6	61	65
Not affected	7	2	9	0	2	20	21
Not applicable	1	1	6	4	0	12	13
Not known	1	0	0	0	0	1	1
	36	29	17	4	8	94	100

The effects on instrumental services were brought about by the mergers, gains and losses of areas which occurred when local government boundaries were rearranged: some LEAs became much larger in size, others diminished, and many former city and borough authorities were swallowed up in the new metropolitan districts or surrounding counties. A third of the LEAs whose services had been affected by the changes reported clear benefits to instrumental music tuition. A similar number suffered distinct disadvantages. The effects in both groups were far-reaching.

Beneficial effects of reorganization included the opportunity to establish or rationalize the instrumental music service. In some LEAs an increase in size brought areas with better provision into what had previously been a less well-resourced authority. Increased size also brought to some an overall expansion of the instrumental teaching force and the chance to offer tuition to more schools and in a wider range of instruments than before. Increased staffing caused some authorities to review the career structure of their instrumental teachers and to appoint more posts at senior levels.

The disadvantages of reorganization were experienced in LEAs which were reduced in size with consequent cuts in their music budget and the loss of staff and resources to neighbouring authorities. Some of these LEAs sustained such substantial losses (for example, one service had its budget cut by 50 per cent) that they dramatically reduced instrumental provision and began charging fees for lessons in school which had hitherto been provided free. Disadvantages were also felt in LEAs which had grown in size without corresponding increases in staff and resources. The intake of areas which formerly had no instrumental music provision put extra strain on existing services and, although some authorities made plans to increase their teaching force, they were unable to do so adequately in the worsening economic climate.

The merging of several former authorities into one often brought with it disparities in provision which have never been evened out. Some LEAs also found themselves with a mixture of two- and three-tier systems, and consequently a different distribution of the service to the schools in each system. In addition, political rivalry and die-hard traditions in some areas have made a more even provision very difficult to achieve. Eighteen authorities in our survey attributed current inequities in the distribution of their service to problems arising from the 1974 reorganization which they have been unable to resolve fully.

The 1980s

The upsurge of interest in wind and brass playing continued and, as Thompson (1985) points out, has, in recent years, become particularly noticeable in the numbers of children learning the flute and clarinet. The increasing popularity of woodwind tuition in schools was reflected in the decision of the National Schools Brass Band Association in 1980 to drop the word 'brass' from its title and to broaden its aims to include the fostering of an interest in music through the playing of brass and woodwind instruments and to the formation of brass and wind bands in schools. The early 1980s also saw the emergence of two new organizations: the World Association for Symphonic Bands and Ensembles (known as WASBE) and the British Association for Symphonic Bands and Wind Ensembles (BASBWE), both of which aimed to advance the status of the wind band and ensemble as a serious and distinctive medium.

In 1981, an event occurred which was to have important implications for the instrumental service in the future. In a test case brought against a local authority which charged for instrumental tuition, the judge ruled that fees should not be imposed for lessons which took place in schools during normal school hours. Asked whether their service had been affected by this judgement, 30 LEAs in our survey replied that it had. Effects were felt mostly by the counties and least by the metropolitan districts and islands (Table 2.3).

The economic cut-backs of the 1970s had encouraged many local authorities to make charges for instrumental tuition and, according to

Table 2.3: *Instrumental music services affected by the 1981 judgement on charges for tuition (94 LEAs)*

Whether affected	English counties	Metropolitan districts	London boroughs	Islands	Wales	No. LEAs	% LEAs
Affected	20	3	5	0	2	30	32
Not affected	16	26	12	4	6	64	68
	36	29	17	4	8	94	100

an article in the Daily Telegraph (Izbicki, 1981), about half of the LEAs in the country were doing so at the time of the test case. Of those taking part in our survey, 27 attributed effects on their service to the fact that they had stopped charging fees and a further three to having been prevented from implementing plans to begin charging.

Ceasing to charge fees in these authorities meant that, unless alternatives could be found, the LEA had either to take over the entire cost of tuition or reduce the service. Some authorities reinstated free tuition; a few undertook most of the cost but asked parents to continue paying on a voluntary basis. Six LEAs reduced their teaching force and the range of instruments taught. Six transferred some of their tuition to the music centres where they could legitimately charge fees out of school hours. Two of these removed tuition from their secondary schools but continued to provide free lessons in primary schools.

The dilemma of trying to provide opportunities for children to learn to play musical instruments, but with limited resources and without recourse to measures which could mean breaking the law, still exists. Indeed, at the time of writing, proposals to clarify the position of LEAs who wish to make charges for various aspects of their instrumental music service form part of a current Government consultation document (GB. DES, 1987b).

The current scene

Recent trends in education

The debate about what, if any, charges should be made for LEA instrumental music tuition is closely bound up with whether instrumental music is perceived to be part of the school curriculum or an optional extra, and whether its purpose is to provide opportunities for all children or to develop the potential of the musically talented.

In 1984, an HMI inquiry into instrumental music provision in England found that in the majority of LEAs instrumental music was considered to be 'an integral part of the curriculum' (GB. DES, 1985a). It also revealed that, although most of the authorities anticipated being able to maintain existing levels of provision, a growing number of activities, including advanced and more specialized tuition, were being moved into the music centres. HMI warned that if charges were to be made, as they legitimately could be for music centre activities, this could cause hardship for certain pupils.

Awareness of the need to provide equal educational opportunities for all children regardless of their social and cultural background has been considerably increased by two major concerns of education in recent years: special educational needs and multicultural provision. The move towards integrating children with special educational needs into mainstream classes has meant that teachers generally are now required to respond to a wide range of pupil need, and the 'unique contribution' which the arts can make in this respect formed one of the main arguments of the Attenborough Report (1985). In the same year, an inquiry into the education of children from ethnic minority groups (Swann Report, 1985) urged educationists to recognize that 'the problem facing the education system is not just how to educate the children of ethnic minorities, but how to educate *all* children'. The need to develop curricula which take account of all children in Britain's culturally diverse society has particular implications for the arts since they provide an opportunity to break out of the Western tradition and introduce children to a wider range of expressive ideas. This opportunity appears to have been taken up more in school-based music than in the instrumental service, although a few authorities have recently expanded their instrumental tuition to include a small range of non-Western instruments. There has also been a growing awareness of the variety of musics which can be made available to young players, such as folk, rock and pop as well as classical and traditional repertoires, and many schools now include drum kits, electric keyboards, synthesizers and computers in their stock of instruments.

The school curriculum and the place of the expressive arts within it have been the subject of much discussion and controversy in recent years. In 1982, the Gulbenkian report 'The Arts in Schools' (Calouste Gulbenkian Foundation, 1982) specifically recommended that 'the arts should be accorded equal status with other major areas of the curriculum and this should be reflected in the allocation of resources'. In the 1985 White Paper 'Better Schools' (GB. DES, 1985b) the Government stated that children should be introduced to 'a range of activities in the arts'. In the same year, the HMI document 'The

Curriculum from 5 to 16' (GB. DES, 1985c) defined aesthetic development as one of nine essential areas of the curriculum and listed art,
music, dance and drama among subjects which contribute particularly
to this area. The document was the second in a series entitled
'Curriculum Matters' and was followed later that year by 'Music from 5
to 16' (GB. DES, 1985d) which set out a framework within which schools
might develop their own music programme. However, concern that the
arts might be squeezed out by other subjects continued to grow as plans
were made for a new national curriculum. In 1987, when the
Government included music and art as foundation subjects in their
National Curriculum proposals, there was both relief that the arts would
have at least a foothold in the curriculum, and concern over the
relatively meagre amount of time left over for them by the core subjects
of maths, English and science.

Meanwhile plans were being made for the new General Certificate of
Secondary Education, the first examinations for which would take place
in the summer of 1988. The GCSE would replace GCE 'O' level and CSE
as a nationwide examination system, and syllabuses would have to
adhere to national criteria. The criteria for music were centred on giving
pupils first-hand experience of listening, composing and performing,
and were expected to cause widespread reappraisal of both curriculum
content and teaching methods. Some teachers welcomed the new
examination because they believed it would match their curriculum
practice more closely than the old system; others were apprehensive
that it would demand competencies which were outside their own
training and experience, especially with regard to composition. There
was clearly a need for sound preparation if the new criteria were to be
met, and at the time of our study the DES-financed 'Cascade' programme of in-service briefing was being undertaken, not without some
haste, with a view to teaching the first course in September 1986.

In this climate of impending change and continuing economic
stringency, many music advisers and senior instrumental staff were
beginning to review their service and consider its future role in
education. Our questionnaire asked them what they believed the main
purposes of an instrumental service should be.

Perceived purposes of the service

In expressing their views on the main purpose of an instrumental
service, respondents to the questionnaire reflected a tension between
the wish to develop potential in the many and pursue excellence in the
few.

Nearly two-thirds of the replies expressed the belief that all or as many children as possible should have access to the service, although some acknowledged the limitations imposed by resources in this respect. By contrast, a substantial minority considered that the service should be directed at children with musical talent, ability or aptitude. This view was expressed mainly in responses from the counties and was scarcely mentioned in replies from other authorities. Between the two extremes, a small group believed that the service should cater for both the broad base *and* the narrower pinnacle of pupil achievement by, for example, offering 'the opportunity of learning an instrument to as many children as possible, and enabling those with talent and commitment to progress to the highest level'.

Although many respondents considered the service to have more than one function, it was possible to group replies according to their main emphases into five categories ranging from a relatively narrow concern with instrumental skills to a wider view of education in general. The perceived purposes of the service can therefore broadly be defined as: teaching specific skills, developing pupil potential, providing experience of music-making, enhancing music education generally and contributing to the all-round development of the individual.

(a)   Teaching specific skills

Despite holding different beliefs about who the service should be for, respondents were agreed that the service should primarily teach the specific skills associated with being able to play an instrument. More than a third declared this to be its main purpose, with the accent on both playing and performance skills. Pupils should be given 'opportunities to experience and develop the playing of an instrument under specialist tuition' and to 'perform with other pupils in ensembles'.

(b)   Developing pupil potential

Nearly a quarter of respondents believed that the development of the pupil's potential should be the main purpose of the service. Most of these were concerned with a particular kind of potential which they described as 'musical talent', 'a special interest and ability', or 'special aptitude'. They believed that the service should, for example, 'help those with obvious musical potential to develop their skills further, fostering and developing musical talent and taking children to as high a standard as possible'.

(c)   Providing experience of music-making

A small group of respondents saw the main purpose of the service as providing opportunities for children to be involved in practical music-making. They emphasized the experience of making music, whether individually or in an ensemble, as an end in itself and believed that the service should give children 'the chance to experience music-making and play with enjoyment'.

(d) Enhancing music education generally

Respondents in this group took a broader view of the instrumental service, placing it in the context of music education as a whole. The purpose of the service was therefore both to support and to enrich the music curriculum; it could also act as a medium through which music education could take place. Seen as an asset not only to the player but also to the school, the service's main purpose is summarized by the adviser who said that 'an instrumental service should develop pupils' skills and experience through a coherent plan for music education'. He went on: 'An instrumental service cannot exist by itself; it has to be part of the music curriculum'.

(e) Contributing to the all-round development of the individual

A small but substantial minority of respondents took a holistic view of education and considered instrumental music in relation to the child's all-round development. From this standpoint, the instrumental service was seen as a part of the whole education service and its staff were perceived to be primarily teachers who could specialize, rather than specialists who could teach. Their task was concerned with the dissemination of knowledge, albeit of a particular kind, which in the process would also enable the child to develop personal qualities such as self-awareness, self-confidence and self-discipline. In learning to play an instrument pupils would 'learn something of themselves', and in playing alongside other pupils they would develop their 'social skills'.

It is not easy to assess how far the perceptions described above are reflected in the actual functioning of individual services. As the case studies showed, the views of the music adviser or head of service responding to this question are not necessarily shared by the staff at the 'chalk face', and even where such views are formulated into policies or guidelines they may not be adhered to by individuals. Secondly, the personal beliefs of the people responsible for running the service may be impossible to put into practice within current economic con-straints. For example, it was the policy in one LEA which had been badly affected by financial cuts to request a 'voluntary contribution' from parents towards the cost of their child's instrumental tuition. In practice, some teachers refused as a matter of principle to collect those contributions and this potential source of income dwindled. Therefore, although senior staff believed that 'the ultimate goal of every LEA should be to give every child the chance to play a musical instrument', they recognized that they could not attempt this within current resources and instead invested the service in children who were considered 'most likely to succeed'.

Local influences

Beliefs about the main purpose of the service may have to be tempered in the light of influences beyond the individual's control. Each instrumental music service is constrained to some extent by the geographical, historical, economic and political factors which obtain in the authority. The operation of the service is likely to be affected by the rural or urban nature of the area and the distribution of the population within it. For example, the logistics of running a service in a group of islands or a large mountainous area of Wales are very different from those in a compact metropolitan district or London borough. The service is also likely to be affected by the authority's musical history and tradition, the availability and accessibility of resources and the priorities of the local council. All these influences conspire to make instrumental music services different from each other, and during our study it became apparent that there are almost as many patterns of provision as there are local authorities.

In addition, there is often variation within an authority between one area and another. Apart from the lingering effects of the 1974 local government reorganization described earlier, more than a quarter of the LEAs in our survey, and in particular the counties, reported factors which made for uneven provision in their authority. The most widespread of these was insufficient staffing, which usually meant that there were not enough specialists to go round and that the service could not be as well-developed in some areas as in others. The second major factor lay in the problems of providing adequately for pupils in rural or less-populated areas. Because there were fewer schools, such areas were more difficult to service and pupil-teacher ratios tended to be larger. Music centres were not likely to be set up in areas where there were insufficient staff and pupils to make them viable. To maximize resources some LEAs concentrated on areas with the largest populations. The population factor created problems in authorities where school rolls had fallen in some areas and risen in others. Attempts to redress imbalances of provision sometimes met with resistance from schools who were unwilling to relinquish some of their allocation so that it could be used elsewhere. Patchy provision also occurred where schools in some areas were supportive of instrumental music and in others were apathetic. A reorganization of the school system had upset the balance in several authorities and the freezing of budgets had prevented any further evening-up of resources.

The picture which emerges is one of variety and diversity. There is no such thing as *the* instrumental music service. Each one is different and indeed has to be if it is to attempt to meet the needs of the children it serves. This chapter has also shown that instrumental music provision in the various LEAs has tended to evolve over the years in a somewhat piecemeal and ad hoc fashion. Many teachers today are faced with a service in which existing practices have developed in response to local traditions and influences. It would seem, therefore, that now more than ever before the time is ripe for each authority to take stock of its provision and consider the principles and purposes underlying its service. Perhaps the findings described in the following chapters will provide a basis for discussion and debate.

3 Staffing and Management

This chapter describes the size and structure of the instrumental teaching force. Changes are noted within the full-time equivalent number of instrumental music staff from 1983 to 1986 and these are discussed with particular reference to regional variations and to fluctuations in the different instrumental groups. The structure of the service is explored in detail in terms of senior and middle management and posts of special responsibility. Attention is then focused on the staff of full-time and part-time teachers and instructors with details of their work, timetables, pay scales and in-service opportunities.

Staffing numbers

Size of instrumental teaching force

The size of the instrumental teaching force varies tremendously from one authority to another. In our survey, figures for the year 1985/6 ranged from a full-time equivalent (FTE) of one teacher in a small island authority to 110 in a large English county.

The questionnaire asked LEAs to state how many full-time equivalent instrumental teaching staff they employed in the years 1983/4 and 1985/6. The intention was to see whether there had been a substantial change in instrumental staffing numbers over the last three years. Not all respondents were able to supply FTE figures for the years requested. However, on the basis of the information provided by 84 authorities it is estimated that about 3,500 FTE teaching staff were employed by LEA instrumental music services in England and Wales in the year 1985/6; of these approximately 3,240 were employed in England and 260 in Wales. In 1984 a small inquiry carried out by HMI reported an FTE of 3,244 instrumental music teachers in England for the year 1983/4. It would therefore appear that the overall size of the country's instrumental teaching force had not changed significantly since then. Nearly half (47 per cent) of the 94 authorities in our survey reported that there had been no change in their FTEs in the last three years; others had sustained gains or losses which, taken together across the whole country, cancelled each other out. Changes in LEAs' instrumental FTEs from 1983/4 to 1985/6 are shown in Table 3.1.

Table 3.1: *Changes in full-time equivalent numbers of instrumental teaching staff from 1983/4 to 1985/6 (94 LEAs)*

	LEAs	
Changes in FTE	No.	%
Remained about the same	44	47
Increased	23	24
Decreased	15	16
Not known	12	13
	94	100

The maintenance by 44 authorities of a stable instrumental FTE over the three-year period is no mean achievement when one takes account of the facts that the economic situation had remained tight and that school rolls were still declining (at the rate of nearly two per cent a year). In real terms stability actually represents an improvement in relation to the total school population. Furthermore, 23 LEAs reported an increase in their FTEs amounting to a total of 37 teachers. Increases were mostly equivalent to one or two teachers, although gains of five and eight had occurred in two authorities which had reorganized their service. Well over half the gains represented increases of three per cent or less in an authority's instrumental staff. Larger gains of five to eight per cent had occurred in nine LEAs: two counties, six metropolitan districts and one London borough. A tenth LEA, one of the smaller London boroughs, had increased its FTE by 25 per cent.

When considering these findings, several points must be borne in mind. Firstly, although 67 responding LEAs had maintained or increased their staffing, some of these still considered themselves to be understaffed. Secondly, losses, though occurring in fewer authorities, were substantial in spite of falling rolls. Fifteen LEAs reported decreases which amounted to a total FTE of between 36 and 37 teachers. Nine of these had sustained losses which represented from five to 13 per cent of their instrumental teaching force, and in one London borough the figure was 29 per cent.

Regional variations

It is interesting to consider the geographic distribution of these changes in staffing. The HMI inquiry of 1984 (*ibid.*) had revealed regional variations and noted that 'a number of LEAs, mainly in the north but including those in the metropolitan division,' had increased their FTE number of instrumental teachers, while 'a small number of LEAs in the southern half of the country' had 'recently made substantial reductions in the number of instrumental teachers employed'. With regard to more recent changes the north-south divide, while still discernible, is no longer so clear-cut. Our survey found that from 1983/4 to 1985/6 increases of five per cent and more were distributed throughout England, occurring in three LEAs in the south, three in the midlands and four in the north. Recent decreases of five per cent and more were also widespread, occurring in five LEAs in the south, one in the midlands and three in the north.

Instrumental groups

Accurate figures for FTE teachers within the different instrumental groups were not always available and some respondents provided approximations. From the information supplied by 84 LEAs it is estimated that about 84 per cent of the FTE staff in England and Wales work in the three main instrumental groups: strings (40 per cent), woodwind (24 per cent) and brass (20 per cent). The rest (16 per cent) teach voice, percussion, harp, guitar, piano, recorders and non-western instruments. The estimated approximate FTE figures for 1985/6 are:

strings	1400
woodwind	840
brass	700
voice and other instruments	560

All responding LEAs employed teachers of brass and woodwind and all but one strings. Teachers of percussion were appointed in two-thirds of authorities, guitar in just over half and piano or keyboards in about a quarter. A small minority of LEAs employed staff to teach (in descending order) recorders, voice, harp, steel pans and other non-western instruments. (Instruments are discussed in detail in Chapter 4, pp. 41-7).

It is not surprising to find that changes in FTE staffing had occurred most in the largest instrumental groups (Table 3.2).

Table 3.2: *Reported changes from 1983/4 to 1985/6 in numbers of full-time equivalent staff teaching various instrumental groups (43 LEAs)*

Instrumental groups	LEAs reporting increases	LEAs reporting decreases	Total reporting changes
woodwind	17	5	22
strings	9	12	21
brass	9	11	20
percussion	8	4	12
guitar	5	4	9
piano/keyboards	1	3	4
voice	1	2	3
non-western	3	0	3
recorders	1	1	2
harp	1	0	1

As the table shows, changes in FTEs were reported for all the instrumental groups. Changes occurred not only in authorities with increased or reduced FTEs but also in LEAs which had maintained their total FTE but had made changes within the various specialisms. Altogether, 43 LEAs reported changes of this kind. Increases had occurred most in woodwind whereas decreases were most common in strings and brass. Both woodwind and percussion had enjoyed more expansions than reductions, and there was an increase in teachers of non-western instruments. In addition, three authorities had expanded their staffing to enable musical support to be given to classroom teachers.

Some respondents were unable to give a detailed breakdown of the numbers of staff teaching each group of instruments. Nevertheless, the information provided by 78 LEAs yielded valuable insights into the nature of staff changes. The number of strings teachers had been increased in some counties and London boroughs but these had been outweighed by reductions in the metropolitan districts. An overall reduction had also been made in teachers of piano/keyboards and voice. Two authorities reported that they had dispensed entirely with the services of their percussion, voice and guitar teachers. Relatively substantial increases had occurred in the numbers teaching woodwind and percussion, with smaller gains and no losses reported for teachers of non-western instruments. Changes in both directions meant that staff numbers remained about the same for brass, guitar and recorders.

Administering the service

The questionnaire sought information on how instrumental music services are administered, and respondents were asked to list in order of seniority the posts of staff involved in running the service in their authority. From this information a number of patterns emerged (see Table 3.3).

The table shows that services varied enormously in the staff administering them, ranging from just one person to a whole panoply of senior and middle management posts. The most common pattern occurring in nearly half (44) of the LEAs in the survey consisted of a music adviser, a head of the instrumental service, and one or more persons with other administrative responsibilities such as area coordinators, music centre leaders and instrumental heads of department. The next most frequent pattern (in 25 LEAs) contained all of these except a separate head of service. At the other extreme were services run by a single person, either the music adviser or someone else specifically appointed to head the service. As the table clearly shows, 13 authorities had no music adviser; two of these had no head of service either and their highest posts were at head of department level.

Senior management

The distribution of senior management posts (advisers and heads of instrumental service) is shown in Table 3.4. Just over half (48) of the LEAs had a head of instrumental music as well as a music adviser, compared with 44 who had either one or the other and two who had neither.

Music advisers

The title 'music adviser' is used here to mean advisers who have specific responsibility for music in an authority. In some LEAs they are designated 'inspectors' or 'inspectors/advisers' but are not to be confused with HMI (Her Majesty's Inspectorate).

Altogether, 86 per cent of the authorities had an adviser or advisers with particular responsibility for music. Those without a music adviser tended to be the smaller authorities: seven metropolitan districts, three London boroughs and two island communities, compared with only one of the counties. Some of these volunteered the information that in their authority instrumental music came under the auspices of the 'director of expressive arts', the 'schools support service' or more commonly a 'general adviser'.

Table 3.3: *Patterns of administration of instrumental music services in 94 LEAs*

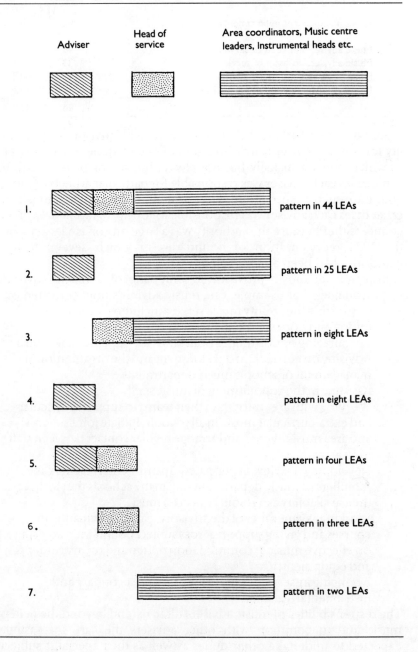

Table 3.4: *Senior management in the instrumental music service (94 LEAs)*

Senior management appointments	LEAs	
	No.	%
Music adviser and head of service	48	51
Music adviser, no head of service	33	35
Head of service, no music adviser	11	12
No head of service, no music adviser	2	2
	94	100

Six authorities had more than one person with advisory responsibility for music. Adviser teams consisted of two or three music advisers of which one was usually but not always the senior or principal. In some cases each adviser was responsible for particular aspects of music education such as curriculum development or instrumental music. In other cases each adviser was responsible for one geographic area of the county, either because the authority was a large one or as a legacy from the 1974 reorganization of boundaries in which several former authorities had been amalgamated.

Instrumental music provision is only one of a music adviser's responsibilities. For example, one music adviser's brief consisted of:

Organizing the county music service including instrumental tuition and associated activities;

Encouraging opportunities of all kinds for pupils to make music;

Advising on curriculum development and the organisation and management of schools music departments;

Assisting in the appointment of music staff;

Working with area tutors and their teams to support curricular and extra-curricular music in all schools, initiate joint schools' and area music events, and arrange regular contact between staff in an area;

Developing the view of peripatetic instrumental teachers as members of music department staff in the schools they visit, and their availability as a resource in class music;

Working as a member of the advisory team, participating in courses and giving support across subject boundaries; advising on effective music accommodation design and on instruments and equipment;

Arranging in-service courses for primary, secondary and instrumental teachers.

The responsibilities of music advisers often extend beyond the field of music and in common with other advisers they are increasingly expected to undertake other duties as well as their specialist subject.

Almost a half of those completing the questionnaire were responsible, in addition to music, for one or more of the following: general advisory work, pastoral care, in-service training, records of achievement, more able children, GCSE, CPVE, libraries, and curricular areas as diverse as media studies, health education and home economics. It is therefore not surprising that the advisers' participation in the instrumental service varies, particularly if there are others involved in running it. For example, in one fairly large authority the adviser delegated the week-by-week running of the service to the director of instrumental music and his team of eleven area directors, assistant directors and heads of department. By contrast, the adviser in a compact urban area with a centrally organized service held regular meetings with staff in both instrumental and general music education and also played an active part in music centre activities.

Heads of instrumental service

The title 'head of instrumental service' is used here to describe an individual, other than an adviser, with overall responsibility for instrumental music in an authority. In practice, designations included the following: head/director/organizer of instrumental service/music/ studies/tuition; director/organizer/head of the (county) music department/school; coordinator for musical activities; head of music support service; senior instrumental tutor/organizer; head of instrumental staff; principal peripatetic/tutor; and tutor-in-charge. Each of these was used to describe the head of the instrumental music service in at least one authority. Similar titles, such as 'senior instrumental teacher', which were sometimes used to describe special posts below the head of service, are not included here.

Sixty-three per cent of the authorities in our survey had a head of instrumental service. All but one of the metropolitan districts had such a post, compared with about half the English counties and London boroughs, and two of the eight Welsh authorities.

There was considerable variety in the level of these posts ranging at the time from Burnham Group 8 down to Scale 1 plus an allowance (see Table 3.5).

The staffing of some instrumental services was clearly structured like that of a school with a head and a series of graded posts. This was said in some areas to be a deliberate policy 'to give the service the status it deserves'. The highest posts for heads of instrumental music (Group 6 and above) were almost all supported by a well-structured team and all had a music adviser. At the other extreme, the Scale 1 post with special allowance was in the country's smallest LEA, where the sole member

Table 3.5:   Heads of instrumental music: level of post in 59 LEAs

Burnham rates	LEAs
Group 8	2
Group 7	5
Group 6	6
Group 5	1
Senior teacher	12
Scale 4	21
Scale 3	10
Scale 2	1
Scale 1 plus allowance	1
	59

of the instrumental service had the task of taking music to the authority's five schools. The Scale 2 post was a part-time one and no one else apart from the adviser was involved in the running of that service. The majority of head-of-service posts however were at the level of Scale 3 and 4 and Senior Teacher. Four authorities also appointed a deputy or assistant to the head of instrumental service.

The nature of the post varied from place to place. From job descriptions made available in the study it was apparent that in administering or assisting the adviser to administer the service, the head of instrumental music was usually expected to take responsibility for arranging team meetings, keeping records, overseeing the instrumental staff, arranging staff timetables, assisting in the appointment of instrumental staff, overseeing the stock of instruments and other equipment, overseeing the music centre(s), establishing examination procedures, identifying staff development and INSET needs, monitoring the quality of the service in schools and music centres, and maintaining a programme of musical performances.

In some LEAs the head of service was also director of the main music centre. Where there was no post of head of service, the music adviser could be adding the above tasks to an already huge commitment. On the other hand, where there was no music adviser, heads of service sometimes found themselves carrying out the entire range of music education duties in the authority.

Some instrumental heads were solely engaged in administering the service while others maintained a considerable teaching load as well. In fact some made a conscious decision to teach for at least part of each week because they felt that this was a valuable way of keeping in touch with the schools.

Middle management

Post-holders described under this heading are those involved in the running of the instrumental service below the level of adviser and head of service and their deputies. They form a bridge between the senior management staff and the rest of the instrumental teaching force. Eighty-four per cent of the LEAs in our survey had staff in this category. Such posts included area heads, music centre leaders, heads of instrumental department (e.g. head of brass), senior instrumental tutors, advisory teachers and others with special responsibilities related to the running of the service. These roles were sometimes combined. For example, an area head might also be the leader of a music centre or head of an instrumental department.

Area heads

This heading refers to posts of responsibility for a geographic area within an authority which were known by various titles including area music heads/directors/coordinators/tutors; senior area instrumental/ music/ peripatetic teachers; and regional instrumental supervisors.

At least 17 authorities had posts of this nature, most of them counties and a few large metropolitan districts where it was practicable to organize the service into separate areas each under its own administrative head. In many cases the job was similar to that of the head of service in a small authority which was organized centrally. Posts ranged in level from Group 4 and Senior Teacher down to Scales 4, 3 and 2. Tasks included responsibility for delivering the instrumental service to the area, overseeing the staff and assisting in appointments, and organizing or checking timetables. In addition, many area heads had responsibility for specific aspects of instrumental music, conducted orchestras, bands and choirs, and taught for a substantial proportion of each week. Some of them managed all this while operating from offices which could only be described as makeshift or on the brink of collapse.

Music centre leaders

All but four of the LEAs in the survey had music centres. Most music centres had their own leader, head or director who was responsible for supervising the staff and activities of the music centre.

In some authorities the instrumental service was administered centrally from a single music centre and its leader might be the adviser or head of service. Other authorities had several music centres, each with its own leader; such appointments were mostly in the range of Scales 2 and 4 or Senior Teacher and were usually held by people who were primarily either instrumental teachers in the service or heads of music departments in schools. The music centre usually functioned as a base for the instrumental service in an area, providing opportunities for children from different schools to meet together in ensembles and choirs. In some cases the so-called 'music centre' was the administrative office only and musical activities actually took place in school premises elsewhere.

The duties of the music centre leaders varied according to the status of the post within the instrumental service and with the uses to which the music centre was put. Basically the leader's job was to ensure the effective and efficient running of the music centre, which usually included supervising the centre's daytime, evening and weekend activities, monitoring the building and its contents, and taking responsibility for the instruments and equipment located there. Where the centre functioned as a base for instrumental teachers the leader might also be responsible for staff timetables, staff meetings, in-service training, pupil courses and performances. (Music centres are discussed in detail in Chapter 7, pp. 108–41).

Heads of instrumental departments

Well over half the authorities in our survey appointed heads of instrumental departments. Most of these were simply designated 'head of...' (brass, strings, etc.), though the following terms were used to describe similar posts in some authorities: senior brass teacher; senior teacher/senior instrumental teacher – brass; supervising/supervisory teacher of brass; and organizer – brass.

The most common pattern was to appoint three heads of department: a head of strings, a head of woodwind, and a head of brass or brass and percussion. Some LEAs appointed only two such posts consisting in all cases of a head of strings, and either a head of brass *or* woodwind or a combination of the two. Others appointed just one head of department; these were *not* all strings posts but ranged across the three main instrumental groups.

A few authorities had more than three heads of department, numbers ranging from mostly four to instances of five, seven and, in one very large authority, twelve. The most common pattern in these cases was to divide strings into upper and lower with a head of each. Other posts were heads of voice or vocal studies, piano, guitar, percussion and steel band.

Heads-of-department posts were in the range of Scale 2 to mostly Scales 3 and 4. Heads of department were expected to take responsibility for the development of instrumental playing across the range of a specified group or groups of instruments. This included being responsible for the appropriate instrumental teachers and their work, overseeing the stock of instruments in the department, arranging courses for pupils, and tutoring ensembles or choirs and the relevant sections of orchestras. In addition, departmental heads usually had a substantial teaching commitment.

Other posts of special responsibility

Posts described under this heading include advisory teachers, senior instrumental tutors, coordinators and 'posts of specific responsibility' other than those already discussed above. They were mostly at the level of Scales 2 and 4 or exceptionally Senior Teacher.

The responsibilities of these post-holders varied according to the structure of the service. For example, one post of senior tutor with responsibility for curriculum and development entailed the oversight of the instrumental curriculum 'in all its aspects, the identification of new developments for the service and its coordination within the general musical life of the authority'. The post-holder was also responsible for 'the organization, administration and programme planning, after due consultation, of all instrumental concerts promoted by the music centres' and for 'the administration of the instrumental staff's car claims and salary claims'. Elsewhere, a senior tutor was appointed with responsibility for community music-making. This post involved the development of an annual music festival as well as small community arts projects. In fact a specific post for the administration and/or direction of orchestras, bands and choirs existed in at least four LEAs.

Not all respondents specified the exact requirements of special posts, but at least two authorities appointed persons with responsibility for arrangement and composition. This involved 'arranging and composing suitable music for ensembles' and in one case also included the administration of a music library. Elsewhere, special posts carried responsibility for resources and in particular the maintenance of a pool of instruments.

29

At least two authorities employed within the instrumental service music coordinators with special responsibility for liaising with primary schools. In one case the coordinator was expected 'to demonstrate to teachers in primary schools the widest possible variety of activities suitable for use in the classroom and to develop an on-going structured programme which teachers may then adapt to suit individual requirements'. He or she was also expected to 'assist those with responsibility for music at primary level in the organization and managerial skills necessary to foster the development of the subject throughout the school.' In addition, this post-holder was required to perform in the peripatetic staff ensemble and to direct an ensemble in a music centre.

A number of other initiatives were in existence including the appointment by one LEA, in partnership with its Regional Arts Association, of a jazz animateur. The post entailed

> the development of jazz improvisation and performance in the youth jazz orchestras and the education sector generally, the composition and arrangement of works for the youth jazz orchestras and other ensembles in the authority, the encouragement of participation in jazz throughout the authority, and the fostering of new jazz venues and promoters.

Nine per cent of LEAs employed a person with responsibility for instrumental music in special schools (schools for children with special educational needs). Although other authorities might have a special needs adviser, or advisory teacher, they did not always involve the instrumental service in their work. Further information on instrumental music in special schools is provided in Chapter 5, pp. 59–60.

Roughly five per cent of LEAs appointed someone with responsibility for ethnic (non-western) instrumental music. One such post-holder, for example, supervised a team of six who taught steel pans, African drums, balalaika, tabla and sitar. Again, some authorities had advisers for multicultural education but did not necessarily involve the instrumental service in their work.

Management structures

From the range of senior and middle management posts described above it is easy to see that instrumental services can differ considerably in the way they are structured from one authority to another. A service rarely, if ever, employs the whole range of post-holders; in fact some services, as we noted earlier, are administered by only one person (see Table 3.3, p.23). However, as the table shows, a total of 82 per cent of the LEAs appointed instrumental staff at senior *and* middle management level. These authorities differed in the way their services were structured but whilst there was considerable variety in detail there were certain basic patterns.

One such pattern was relatively simple (Figure 3.1). Instrumental music was organized by the music adviser, the head of service and the heads of department (usually brass, woodwind and strings). The instrumental teachers were responsible to the heads of department who in turn were responsible to the head of service who was answerable to the adviser. The organizational structure was thus a very clear one. It occurred in compact areas where the service was organized centrally.

A more complex structure (Figure 3.2) took account of the fact that the instrumental service was administered in distinct geographical areas. Each area was organized by an area coordinator and contained one or more music centres each with its own leader. Again, the structure was a very clear one. The instrumental teachers were responsible to the leader of the music centre at which they were based, who in turn was responsible to the area coordinator and so on. Services organized along these lines occurred in the larger authorities, particularly counties, where it was considered more practical to administer in areas rather than centrally. Some of these also employed heads of department whose work was not confined to specific geographical areas but covered the whole authority.

The teachers

Instrumental staff have a variety of qualifications. Most have trained with a specialism in music and many also have qualified teacher status (QTS). Qualified teacher status is accorded to those who hold a DES-approved teaching qualification, currently the Bachelor of Education degree (BEd) or the Post-Graduate Certificate in Education (PGCE) or equivalent. Instrumental teachers who do not have these qualifications are usually called 'instructors'. They often hold a degree in music and a teaching diploma gained at a music college. Most authorities employ a mixture of teachers and instructors though, as some pointed out, they are now tending to appoint 'suitable qualified teachers' in preference to instructors.

Discrepancies in pay and career prospects between instrumental teachers with and without QTS have for many years caused concern in the profession, and various attempts have been made to improve the situation. For example, in 1983 the European String Teachers

Figure 3.1:   *Example of a management structure in a centrally administered instrumental service*

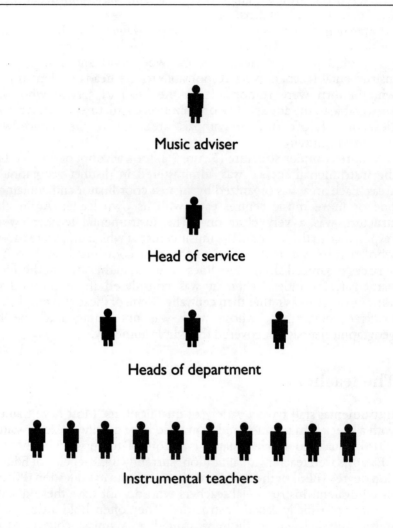

Music adviser

Head of service

Heads of department

Instrumental teachers

Figure 3.2: *Example of a management structure in an area-administered instrumental service*

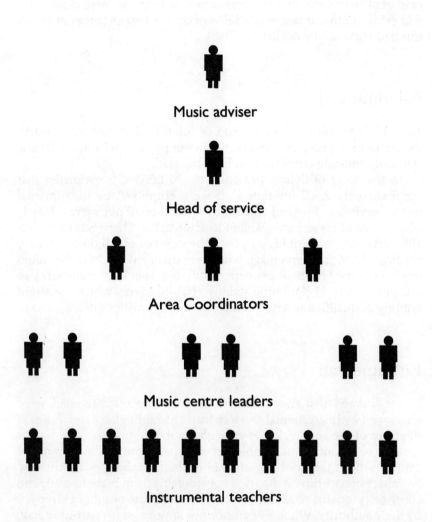

Music adviser

Head of service

Area Coordinators

Music centre leaders

Instrumental teachers

Association (ESTA) produced a report which, while recommending that routes into professional teaching should remain diverse, called for more 'opportunity for instructors to acquire Qualified Teacher Status, either through attendance at special courses or through special case representation by the local music adviser or inspector'. Ther was evidence in our case-study LEAs of one or two instances in which this had successfully occurred.

Full-time staff

Most LEAs employ a combination of full-time and part-time instrumental teaching staff. Five authorities in our survey appointed full-time staff *only* and one employed *no* full-time staff.

On the basis of figures provided by 90 LEAs it is estimated that approximately 2,500 full-time staff were employed by instrumental music services in England and Wales at the time of our survey. Nearly 80 per cent of these had qualified teacher status. There was considerable variation between LEAs in both the number of full-time staff they employed and the percentage who were qualified teachers. Qualified teachers ranged from 18 per cent of full-time staff in one authority to 100 per cent in 14. Full-time staffing establishments which consisted entirely of qualified teachers tended to be the smaller ones.

Part-time staff

It is estimated that more than 4,000 part-time teaching staff were employed by instrumental services throughout England and Wales at the time of the survey. It was difficult to obtain more precise figures because some authorities employed extra part-time staff in their music centres whom they did not include in their teaching establishment. Numbers of part-time staff varied considerably from place to place and some respondents could only hazard a guess at the number employed by their authority. While five authorities appointed no part-time staff, those at the other extreme employed huge numbers of part-timers (around 200 in one county and 1100 in a large London borough) to supplement a very small full-time staff. Job-sharing was also in evidence in some places.

In our survey just under a quarter of part-time staff were qualified teachers. Again proportions varied from one authority to another; in two LEAs all the part-time staff were qualified teachers and in one of these every member of the instrumental teaching force, both full and part-time, had qualified teacher status.

The nature of the job

At the time of the survey only a small minority (17 per cent) of LEAs provided a written job description for all their instrumental staff. It was more common to supply a job description for full-time staff only: about one in four LEAs did this. A third of the authorities provided no job description at all for any of their staff, and more than two-thirds (70 per cent) provided nothing for their part-timers. The pattern seemed to be that if there was a job description for part-timers there was one for everyone; if there was nothing for full-timers there was nothing for anyone.

In some cases job descriptions were provided only for the more senior posts. In a few authorities the matter was under review and one or two commented that all newly-appointed staff would have a job description in future.

The responsibilities of full-time instrumental staff usually entailed teaching individuals and groups of children in primary and secondary schools, coaching ensembles, bands and orchestras, and participating in the work of the music centre. Staff were expected to work closely with headteachers and music teachers in the schools, and might also be required to take part in staff recitals and workshops. The job called for flexible timetabling: music centre activities mostly took place outside school hours, usually in the evenings and on Saturdays, and some authorities also required participation in pupil courses held during school holidays for which time in lieu might be given. Additional requirements to attend music centre and other activities might be awarded an extra payment on an hourly basis.

Many instrumental teachers are expected to travel to a number of schools over distances which usually require the use of a car (for which an 'essential users' allowance may be paid). Although efforts are made to restrict the area covered by any one teacher, the geographical nature of some LEAs is such that distances between schools may be relatively large. Journeys tended to be longer for specialist teachers of minority instruments such as oboe, bassoon and double-bass because they had to reach fewer pupils in a greater number of schools. Most authorities (84 per cent) made an allowance for travelling time in staff timetables, although some stipulated the distances which merited the allowance.

Other timetabling allowances were sometimes made. For example, two-thirds of LEAs allowed time for at least some of their teachers to give recitals in schools. These might take place on a regular basis such as half a day per week or be given at certain points in the term. A few authorities (14 per cent) gave staff a certain amount of lesson preparation time. This allowance was made in some cases to probationer teachers only or to those who rehearsed orchestras and ensembles for no extra payment. A very small minority (three per cent) allowed practice time. On the other hand, eight authorities made no timetabling allowances of any kind. However, it was anticipated that the new Conditions of Employment for Teachers would clarify the position with regard to what should count as 'working time'.

Pay structure

At the time of the survey Burnham Scales for teachers were still in operation. Eighty-eight LEAs provided information on pay structures for their instrumental music teachers. These varied between authorities and, excluding the senior and management posts discussed earlier, ranged across Burnham Scales 1 to 3 with, in some LEAs, different scales for instructors. Well over a third (34) of the LEAs placed all or most of their full-time instrumental teachers on Scale 2. A quarter (23) of the authorities employed a mixture of Scale 1 and 2 teachers, and a further quarter (22) paid them all or mostly on Scale 1. A small minority also included a few Scale 3 appointments. Exceptionally, two LEAs placed a substantial proportion of their full-time teachers on Scale 3; in both cases the entire service was clearly structured into successive levels from Scales 1 to 4, thereby implying a progressive career structure. When the survey was carried out, the question of a career structure for instrumental teachers was one which was attracting increasing attention, and in some areas working parties had been formed to assess the situation and to discuss related issues such as conditions of service and teacher appraisal.

Rates for instructors varied: some LEAs placed them on Burnham Scales 1 or 2 with a bar towards the upper end of the scale; others paid them on the DES-approved Instructor Scales A to D or at a point between Scale A and Scale 1. Some authorities paid a special instructors' rate which, depending on the authority, might for example be 'related to Scale 2', 'equivalent to Scale 1' or an 'agreed instructors' scale'.

Part-time staff were either salaried or, more commonly, employed on an hourly basis. Fewer than a quarter of LEAs appointing part-timers paid them a salary, compared with more than half paying an hourly rate and the rest paying a mixture of salaries and hourly rates. The decision to pay a salary or an hourly rate depended in some authorities on whether the employee was a qualified teacher or not and in others on the number of hours worked.

After the survey was carried out, new legislation was made on teachers' pay and working hours (GB.DES, 1987a) which could have important implications for instrumental music staff. The former Burnham Scales for teachers other than Heads and deputies were to be replaced by a single scale (Appendix, p.159). Full-time teachers would be required to work at the direction of the head teacher or the authority for '1,265 hours in any year', and would be 'available for work for 195 days in any year', of which 190 days would be days on which they 'may be required to teach pupils in addition to carrying out other duties' (para. 36.1).

In-service training

Most LEAs (85 per cent of those in our survey) provided some form of in-service training for instrumental staff. A substantial minority how-ever made no such provision; this was particularly noticeable among the London boroughs. The vast majority provided courses or meet-ings of more general interest to all instrumental staff and of particular interest to specific instrumental groups. About two-thirds also organized opportunities for instrumental staff and school-based music teachers to attend courses together. However, in-service training for instrumental teachers was not as well-developed as it may seem: many respondents commented that such opportunities were not a regular occurrence but happened 'occasionally' or 'rarely'. One or two also made the point that it was difficult to persuade part-time staff to attend without paying them extra to do so.

Respondents mentioned that it can be difficult and expensive to organize in-service opportunities for an instrumental teaching force which is small in number. Some authorities solved this problem by linking with their neighbours or by arranging for their staff to attend courses elsewhere.

One LEA provided in-service meetings for the whole of its 'schools support services' including teams of teachers working in language development, multicultural education, maths, science, for-eign languages, computers and drugs education as well as the expressive arts.

Another difficulty is that secondment is not usually available to instrumental staff in the way that it is for other teachers. Some authorities provided in-service meetings for peripatetic tutors during a time when it was impracticable for them to go into schools, such as the first few days of term. Such meetings might include administrative matters, staff discussions and a talk by a prominent speaker. Some instrumental teachers told us that they sometimes found such talks to be irrelevant to their own needs and therefore felt they were wasting precious time. To help overcome this at least one service had a working-party which met regularly to discuss in-service needs. Suggestions resulted in a two-day course on the topic of liaising with schools, a workshop on composition, and a range of talks given by advisory teachers on, for example, multicultural and special educational needs. There was also considered to be a need among post-holders for a management course, a topic taken up by one of the regional branches of MANA (the Music Advisers' National Association) which in 1987 organized a three-day residential course for staff in its constituent local authorities. Some staff stressed the isolation of the peripatetic teacher and the need for more in-service support. One service had devised a system of pairing teachers so that they could critically appraise each other's work. Despite initial misgivings the scheme was an agreed success and not only enabled teachers to learn from each other but also encouraged them to appraise their own work. Staff in other areas told us that they would appreciate discussion on methods and techniques, partly to give them more confidence in their own teaching and partly to stimulate new ideas. Highly specialist master classes would also be welcomed.

Some teachers said they would like to hear what went on outside their own authority and indeed in other countries. All but two LEAs gave financial assistance to instrumental teachers wishing to attend courses or conferences organized by agencies other than the authority, though some limited this assistance by offering it to full-time staff only.

A discussion of INSET for instrumental teachers would not be complete without pointing out the part that the instrumental service can play in the in-service training of classroom teachers. Instrumental teachers have a lot to offer in terms of their specialist musical skills and are perhaps an under-used resource in the training of other teachers. A small but increasing number of authorities were involving or planning to involve instrumental staff in a supportive or advisory capacity to work alongside classroom teachers in their school. (The integration of instrumental and classroom music is addressed in more detail in Chapter 6, pp. 100–5).

Summary

The findings suggest that since 1983 the overall size of the instrumental teaching force in England and Wales has remained about the same, despite the fact that rolls have continued to fall. This apparent stability must, however, be treated with caution. First, a number of LEAs have experienced changes in their instrumental FTEs and losses, while less widespread, have been more substantial than gains. Secondly, despite the encouraging number of LEAs which have increased or maintained their numbers, staffing levels even in these authorities are often still insufficient to meet demand.

Instrumental teachers are concentrated largely in three main instrumental groups: strings, woodwind and brass. Only a relatively small proportion (16 per cent) teach instruments other than these, including the voice. It is estimated that there are twice as many strings teachers as brass, with woodwind in between. Fluctuations within the various instrumental groups reveal interesting trends. From 1983/4 to 1985/6 increases in FTEs occurred most widely in woodwind, whereas decreases were made most widely in strings and brass. On a lesser scale, there had been more gains than losses in teachers of percussion, guitar, harp and non-western instruments, whereas the opposite was true for piano and voice.

The way in which the service is administered depends very much on local factors, and there is considerable variety in the way the service is structured in different LEAs. Seven patterns of administration were found, ranging from services with a clear hierarchical structure to those run by a single member of staff. The most common pattern consisted of the adviser and head of service at the top with a middle management team of coordinators, music centre leaders and heads of department. Within the various administrative patterns there was considerable variety of detail. For example some services, particularly in the more compact urban areas, were administered centrally and functioned as a single entity whereas others, especially in the larger counties, were organized into separate geographical areas, each with its own structure. In either case, staff were ultimately responsible to the music adviser if there was one or to the head of instrumental service. However, 14 per cent of the LEAs had no music adviser and 37 per cent had no head of service. Two per cent had neither an adviser nor a head of service.

It is estimated that, at the time of the survey, approximately 2,500 full-time and 4,000 part-time staff were employed by LEA instrumental music services in England and Wales. Most authorities employ a mixture of full-and part-time staff. The survey revealed that nearly 80 per cent of full-time staff had qualified teacher status compared with 24 per cent of part-timers. There has been a tendency recently in some authorities to appoint qualified teachers in preference to instructors. This, coupled with the move towards a more structured service, was seen to be a means of giving instrumental music a higher profile and strengthening its position in relation to the school curriculum.

Recent legislation on new pay and contractual arrangements for teachers has focused attention on the need for a clearer career structure for instrumental staff. It has also provided opportunities to clarify their role. At the time of the survey only 17 per cent of LEAs provided a written job description for all their instrumental staff, but there were signs that the matter was increasingly coming under review.

Rates of pay for both teachers and instructors were found to vary quite substantially between LEAs, and the new pay scales offer authorities an opportunity to reappraise this situation. There is also a need to review in-service provision for instrumental staff, particularly where plans are being made to integrate the service more closely with classroom music. Although 85 per cent of LEAs provided some form of INSET for instrumental teachers, much of this was of an occasional nature and did not form part of a coherent programme of training. The difficulties of organizing in-service opportunities for a relatively small and specialized section of the teaching force, many of whom are employed on an hourly rather than a salaried basis, need to be taken into account. Moreover, it should not be forgotten that there is scope for instrumental staff to play an active role in the in-service training and support of teachers in the classroom.

4 Instruments and Resources

This chapter describes the range of instruments taught through the instrumental music service, and considers who provides the instruments and what arrangements are made for their loan, hire or purchase. The financial resourcing of the service is then discussed in terms of budgets and expenditure and the areas to which parents are expected or invited to contribute.

The instruments

Range of instruments taught

The range of instruments covered and the extent to which they were being taught throughout England and Wales at the time of the survey are shown in Table 4.1. Of the 94 LEAs responding to the questionnaire one was unable to supply this information; the table is therefore based on details from 93 authorities.

As one would expect, the main orchestral groups of instruments (woodwind, brass and strings) were taught in all or almost all the LEAs in our survey. Of the wind instruments tuition in the flute, clarinet, oboe and bassoon was provided in every authority; the same was true of brass instruments for trumpet, horn and trombone. Of the strings violin, viola and cello were taught in all but one exceptionally small LEA which had only one instrumental teacher. Saxophone, tuba and double bass were also taught almost everywhere. In addition, tuition on instruments such as cor anglais and bass clarinet was given to more advanced pupils when required for special performances. The great majority of instrumental services also provided tuition in brass band and percussion, and more than two-thirds taught classical guitar.

Table 4.1:   Instruments taught through the instrumental music service (93* LEAs)

Instruments	% LEAs
flute	100
clarinet	100
oboe	100
bassoon	100
trumpet	100
horn	100
trombone	100
violin	99
viola	99
cello	99
saxophone	99
tuba	99
double bass	98
brass band instruments	90
percussion	86
guitar (classical)	68
recorders	48
piano	38
guitar (electric/bass)	33
synthesizer/electric keyboards	30
voice	27
harp	24
early instruments (other than recorder)	19
steel band	18
sitar	8
tabla	8
harmonium	8
other non-Western instruments	2
other instruments	9

* One responding LEA did not provide this information.

Although the recorder is very widely taught by classroom teachers especially at the primary level, nearly half the authorities made provision for recorder teaching through their instrumental service, offering more advanced tuition and opportunities to play in consort. Other early musical instruments were taught on a smaller scale: nearly a fifth of authorities provided some tuition in early instruments though none of these was in Wales. On the other hand every Welsh LEA taught the harp, an instrument which was included by 16 per cent of authorities in England. Some respondents made the point that instruments such as harps and bassoons were available but they lacked the specialists to teach them.

The service provided piano tuition in over a third of LEAs; by comparison nearly as many taught popular modern instruments like the electric or bass guitar, synthesizer and electric keyboards. Senior staff in various parts of the country explained that, although there was a demand, piano tuition was not encouraged in their authority and was even being phased out in some LEAs. Several reasons were given for this. Despite the work of Yvonne Enoch and others who advocate group piano teaching, learning to play the piano is still widely perceived as an individual activity which does not accord with the policies of many LEAs on group tuition. Secondly, the piano is an expensive instrument which, as one adviser said, 'soaks up too much of the budget'. Some authorities offered the piano as a second study only; others planned to increase pupils' opportunities to work on electric keyboards instead. Electronic instruments were increasingly being used by school-based teachers, even where they were not taught through the instrumental service.

Just over a quarter of LEAs offered voice or choral tuition. Senior staff spoke of the 'sad omission' of vocal work in their authorities and blamed this situation on the widely held but mistaken view that anyone can sing and therefore tuition is neither as necessary nor as important as it is for other instruments. Although some believe that the *training* of the voice is probably best left until the age of 18, others feel strongly that much valuable work can be done earlier in teaching children how to *use* their voices. One respondent explained that school choirs seemed to be 'out of fashion' in her authority and there was a need particularly to overcome a tremendous shortage of boy singers.

Although non-Western instruments are used in class-based music in some areas, opportunities for learning to play them through the instrumental service were found to be few and far between. Steel pans were twice as likely to be taught as instruments of Asian origin: sitar, tabla and harmonium tuition occurred on a small scale in seven responding authorities in England and none in Wales. Other non-Western provision included the Indian flute in one authority and the balalaika and African drums in another. Several heads of service added that they would like to include Chinese musical instruments if resources allowed. In one LEA the instrumental service operated a multicultural unit with six teachers of Indian instruments, steel band, African drum and balalaika. As well as teaching these instruments throughout the authority, the team were involved in school-based curriculum projects where they offered six-week taster courses so the children could try out the various instruments.

Some advisers explained that they were deliberately trying to move away from the Western instrumental tradition into a more multicultural approach. Several pointed out that a multicultural approach does not necessarily involve ethnic instrumental tuition. They considered it more important to acquaint children with the richness and variety of music from different cultures than to teach them to play ethnic instruments; in fact this was already being attempted in many areas through classroom-based music and the use of projects and themes. It was widely acknowledged that, while it is important for children to appreciate the music of other cultures, non-Western instruments 'with their different scales and tonalities' can be very difficult to teach, especially to 'Western ears'. The recruitment of specialists to teach such instruments was also felt to be a difficult task, and in some areas the teaching of Indian or Afro-Caribbean instruments was entirely due to the fortuitous presence of talented and willing parents.

A few LEAs provided for instruments which were not apparently taught anywhere else. For example, the organ, folk guitar, accordion and Northumbrian pipes were each mentioned by only one respondent in our survey. In addition to instrumental tuition, at least two services made special provision for young children (of three to seven or so) to gain grounding in musical literacy. Based on the work of Kodaly and Orff, such courses aimed to supplement the work done in the classroom and sought to establish a sense of pitch and rhythm through movement to music, singing games and the use of tuned and untuned percussion. At the other end of the age-range one service offered tuition in sound-recording for pupils of sixteen and over.

Where the instruments were taught

The location of LEA tuition in the various instruments is shown in Table 4.2. The table shows that most instrumental teaching took place in schools. Most of the instruments listed were taught either solely in schools or in both schools and music centres. (All but four of the LEAs had music centres.) By contrast there were some instruments, notably percussion, for which a minority of LEAs located tuition only in their music centres, often for practical reasons.

Where the instruments come from

Instruments used by the instrumental teaching service come from two main sources: the local authority and the pupils (or, more precisely, their parents). In 68 per cent of the authorities in our survey instruments were largely purchased by the LEA. This was done mainly from centrally-administered funds which were, in many cases, supplemented by school capitations. Fifty-seven per cent provided the bulk of their instruments from central funds. The proportion of instruments purchased for the service from school capitations was in most cases relatively small, usually no more than one-fifth of the instruments in use. A minority of LEAs relied more heavily on the schools and,

Table 4.2: *Where instruments were taught through the instrumental music service (93* LEAs)*

Instruments	In schools only	In music centres only	In schools and music centres	Total
flute	51	0	42	93
clarinet	52	0	41	93
oboe	56	2	35	93
bassoon	55	5	33	93
trumpet	52	0	41	93
horn	53	4	36	93
trombone	52	0	41	93
violin	49	0	43	92
viola	54	0	38	92
cello	49	0	43	92
saxophone	51	4	37	92
tuba	60	0	32	92
double bass	47	5	39	91
brass band	49	1	34	84
percussion	33	18	29	80
guitar (classical)	34	7	22	63
recorders	21	12	12	45
piano	14	9	12	35
guitar (electric/bass)	13	11	7	31
synthesizer/electric keyboards	19	1	8	28
voice	11	6	8	25
harp	13	6	3	22
early instruments	8	8	2	18
steel band	12	0	5	17
sitar	4	1	2	7
tabla	4	1	2	7
harmonium	3	2	2	7

* One responding LEA did not provide this information
Four LEAs had no music centres

exceptionally, in one authority all the instruments were purchased in this way. By comparison, in 28 per cent of the authorities instruments were mostly purchased by individual pupils. It should also be mentioned that in some areas parent support groups were an additional source of provision, supplying funds to buy the more specialist or more expensive instruments. (Parent support groups are discussed in more detail in Chapter 7, pp. 135–8).

Arrangements made for the purchase and allocation of instruments can indicate an authority's attitude towards and resources for its instrumental teaching service. At one extreme are the authorities in which almost all the instruments are provided by the LEA and are loaned to pupils free of charge for an unlimited period. At the other extreme are the authorities in which almost all the instruments are provided by individual pupils and such LEA stocks as exist are hired out to pupils for a fee and for a limited period only. These and the various groups in between are shown in Table 4.3.

Table 4.3: *Where the instruments came from (94 LEAs)*

Purchase and allocation arrangements	% LEAs
Mostly purchased by the LEA and lent to pupils free of charge for an unlimited period; pupils may or may not be encouraged to buy their own eventually.	38
Mostly purchased by the LEA and lent to pupils free of charge for a limited period; pupils then encouraged to buy their own.	26
Mostly purchased by the LEA and hired to pupils for a fee.	4
Evenly purchased by the LEA and the pupils; LEA stocks lent to pupils free of charge.	4
Mostly purchased by individual pupils; LEA stocks lent to pupils free of charge.	21
Mostly purchased by individual pupils; LEA stocks hired to pupils for a fee.	7
	100

As the table shows, well over a third of the LEAs not only provided most of the instruments but loaned them to pupils free of charge for an unlimited period. Fifteen of these made no stipulation as to when pupils might eventually supply their own instrument. The other authorities in this group encouraged parents to buy an instrument when their child had reached a certain stage, though exceptions were usually made in cases of financial hardship. About a quarter of LEAs took this a step further by lending instruments for a limited period only; at the end of this time parents were encouraged or, in some cases, expected to provide an instrument on which their child could continue. This procedure ensures that LEA instruments are released and available for the next set of beginners.

The stage at which parents were encouraged to buy an instrument varied quite widely. Where loans were made for a limited period only, this stage was defined quite clearly: most commonly after one or two years' tuition. In other authorities the stage was defined in terms of the child's age: on transfer from primary to secondary school or at age 13–14. In some areas the lending period differed according to the instrument, for example six months for the less expensive flute, clarinet and trumpet and several years for the more costly bassoon or tuba. The limit on the loan of strings was usually reached when a full-size instrument was required.

A small minority of LEAs required children to provide their own instrument from the start or as soon as possible. At the other extreme were those who encouraged pupils to buy an instrument towards the end of their schooling. One such authority, which provided instruments free for an unlimited period, had devised a scheme whereby pupils could, if they wished, purchase an instrument in instalments over their last two years in school. This avoided the situation where children who had been receiving tuition for a long time might suddenly find themselves bereft of an instrument on leaving school.

Some authorities set flexible limits on the lending period, recommending that pupils buy their own instrument only when they had shown 'evidence of commitment' and sustained 'some degree of progress'. It was often left to the discretion of the instrumental teacher to determine when this stage had been reached. One or two LEAs suggested waiting until the child would benefit from individual tuition or from playing an instrument of better quality. In some areas parents were encouraged to rent instruments commercially rather than buy them during the early stages of tuition. In other areas there were schemes through which instruments hired to pupils by the service might eventually be purchased.

Financial resources

Budgets

The instrumental music service had its own budget allocation in more than three-quarters (73) of the LEAs in our survey. In eight more authorities the service was funded as part of the authority's general music budget which was administered by the music adviser. The allocation of money for the instrumental service in some areas was quite complex with sums being apportioned in a variety of ways. For example, while instrumental teaching staff were often paid from central staffing funds, the instruments might be purchased from the music adviser's budget, courses supported from an overall vote for musical activities and transport costs borne by a 'special' vote. At the time of the survey, one authority allocated a sum of money to each school which could be used at the head's discretion for a variety of purposes including the employment of instrumental teachers.

Four authorities allocated no special budget to the service as such but funded their music centres either with a lump sum or with separate capitation allowances like schools. Three more set aside a specific amount just for concerts and other special events. Some instrumental services were financed on an indirect basis, relying on votes or bids from a general LEA fund such as 'curriculum development', 'support' or 'supplies'. In one case, the teacher responsible for the instrumental service reported that he personally received no budget but relied on 'random small windfalls'.

Here are examples of the ways in which the instrumental music service is financed in two very different authorities. The first is a metropolitan district in which the service is organized centrally from the music school (or music centre). Education has a high priority in this LEA and music is well-resourced. All tuition is free and instruments are provided and maintained free of charge. The instrumental service has its own budget which is used for the purchase, replacement and repair of instruments and other equipment. The service also provides free transport to the music school, and supports tuition at master classes and attendances at junior departments of colleges of music by paying half the travel and fee. There is no charge for attending the music school. The head of the music school retains some of the instrument budget for repairs; the rest is shared between the three curriculum heads who are responsible for ordering instruments within their own departments.

The second example is a large county in which the instrumental service is organized into areas. It illustrates disparate sources of funding. Money for the instrumental service comes from two main sources. One is the authority's 'curriculum development fund' which is channelled through the chief inspector and allocated to the various subject areas. Amounts are relatively very small, so the sum received for music is usually concentrated on one particular school or project. The other source is the 'replacement of equipment fund' which is used to buy the more expensive orchestral instruments and to replace some of the worn-out pianos with electric keyboards and synthesizers. Sums are allotted to each of the six areas of the county for the purchase and repair of instruments and equipment, and area music centres also receive an amount to cover stationery and sheet music for ensembles. Although participation in ensembles is free, a charge is made for music centre tuition, and about 40 per cent of the instruments used in this service are provided by the pupils.

Allowing for inflation, 50 per cent of the LEAs in our survey reported that sums of money allocated to their instrumental service in the year 1985/6 had remained about the same as in the previous year; 45 per cent had experienced changes from one year to the next. A comparison between budgets from 1985/6 and the previous year is shown in Table 4.4.

Table 4.4: *A comparison between budgets allocated to the instrumental music service in 1985/6 and in the previous year (94 LEAs)*

Allowing for inflation	% LEAs
Budget remained unchanged	50
Budget represented an increase	27
Budget represented a decrease	18
Not known	5
	100

The table shows that more than a quarter of the LEAs reported an increase in funding for their instrumental service. The English counties were particularly well-represented in this group: one in three stated that allocations had improved. By contrast, 18 per cent of LEAs reported a decrease in funding. This was especially noticeable in the metropolitan districts where one in three had had their allocations reduced.

Expenditure

The survey sought information on whether LEAs had spent money in 1985/6 on items such as instrumental repairs and the purchase of instruments, sheet music and other equipment. The findings are presented in Table 4.5.

As one might expect, the repair and maintenance of instruments was an object of expenditure in almost every LEA. The few who did not spend anything on this were all authorities in which most of the

Table 4.5: *Items of expenditure from instrumental music budgets in 1985/6 (94 LEAs)*

Item	% LEAs
Repair and maintenance of instruments	91
Music for groups and ensembles	87
Purchase of equipment (e.g. music stands)	81
Purchase of instruments	80
Music for individual use	43
Not known	5

instruments were owned by the pupils and LEA stocks very small. Well over a third of LEAs (37) asked parents for a contribution towards the maintenance and repair of authority-owned instruments used by their children. These included not only authorities who lent instruments to children free of charge but also some of those who hired instruments to pupils for a fee. Contributions varied: for example, £2.95 per annum in one authority and £9.75 in another. On the other hand, nearly two-thirds (57) of LEAs, in particular many metropolitan districts, made no such request except perhaps where damage was clearly caused by extreme negligence.

Instrumental repairs can be time-consuming, labour-intensive and costly, and authorities had various strategies for coping with them. Centrally-owned stocks might be maintained from a special repair fund or by the schools, while school-owned instruments were sometimes covered by capitation. One authority which provided all the instruments free of charge had its own workshop employing a technician to carry out all but the most specialized repairs. Another authority which encouraged pupils to buy their own instruments directed parents to suitable sources for repairs and accessories; it also provided them with guidance on insuring and caring for their instruments.

The next most widespread item of expenditure was the buying or hiring of music for groups and ensembles. This was closely followed by the purchase of instruments and related equipment such as music stands. Given that most musical instruments are costly, it is perhaps to their credit that so many services managed to replenish or even expand their stocks. A survey of LEA music funding carried out in 1984 by the Federation of Music Industries found that only one per cent of respondents planned not to buy any instruments that year, whereas our own survey found that in 1985/6 15 per cent spent nothing on this item. Some advisers explained that with ever-rising prices and a standstill budget it was difficult to replace instruments at all let alone improve on their quality. They pointed out that, while councils enjoyed the 'window-dressing' activities of prestige youth orchestras and bands, they sometimes failed to realize the cost of resourcing them, and the need to buy instruments was in constant competition with necessary and worthwhile initiatives in other fields.

Music for individual use, which can be costly on a large scale, was the item least frequently purchased by the authorities. Well over half of them spent nothing on this in 1985/6, the reason being that most authorities (88 per cent of those in our survey) asked parents to buy music for their child. In some cases this applied to all the music the child would need including tutor books, studies, sheet music and examination material; in others, some of the music was provided by the schools or music centres. A few authorities were opposed to asking for contributions of this nature. Indeed one adviser expressed the view that music is as much a part of the curriculum as maths and English, and therefore children should no more be required to provide music books than they are expected to buy their own textbooks.

Whether they agreed with this view or not, there were clearly many advisers and heads of service who felt that the only way they could obtain adequate resources for their service was by asking parents to help them. Apart from the items already discussed, 41 per cent of authorities welcomed parental contributions towards at least one of the following:

the purchase of sundries such as reeds, strings, shoulder pads and rosin;

the cost of their child's participation in courses, workshops and tours;

out-of-school tuition especially at music centres (see Chapter 7, pp. 108–41 for details);

membership of area or authority-wide orchestras, choirs and ensembles;

transport to and from rehearsals;

external examination fees.

In some areas parent support groups such as 'The Friends of the Youth Orchestra' engaged in voluntary fund-raising activities. Music centres were often the focus of such groups and these are discussed in more detail in Chapter 7, pp. 108–41. Special events such as end-of-term concerts could also bring in small amounts in the form of a nominal entry or programme charge.

Five authorities accepted voluntary contributions or donations towards the cost of running the instrumental music service. All of these were charging fees for instrumental tuition in schools up until the legal judgment of 1981 when this practice was ruled out. They then asked parents to continue making a contribution or donation on a voluntary basis. In some areas parents were willing to do this and in one LEA it was estimated that as many as 80 per cent of the parents still made such a contribution. However, another authority found that voluntary contributions dwindled over the years, a fact which the music adviser took to be indicative of waning interest and support. He considered instrumental provision to be the most costly and vulnerable sector of the education service, and feared that the authority might perhaps one day wonder why they should maintain an expensive service when parents were unwilling to show even token support. Parents, on the other hand, may not wish to pay extra for something which they see to be part of their child's schooling. Charges may legitimately be charged for out-of-school tuition, notably at music centres and, while not all LEAs made such a charge, some advisers were of the opinion that, in order to meet costs, instrumental tuition in their authority might eventually have to be removed from the schools and be located entirely in music centres.

Two of the authorities requesting donations did not in fact have any music centres, and used the money to buy instruments and extra teaching time. A third authority asked for what it called 'a nominal contribution' towards tuition; the same parents also paid a hire fee for their children to use LEA instruments which could eventually be purchased. All these costs were justified on the grounds that demand far exceeded supply and this was a way of meeting that demand. However, it also raises questions about opportunities for children whose parents are unwilling or unable to pay and the social pressures which might be upon them in an area where the majority do comply. As the adviser of one such LEA commented: 'Eighty-three per cent of our instrumental tuition is taken up by the middle-class prosperous south of the authority compared with 17 per cent in the poorer north.'

Summary

The survey revealed that the main orchestral groups of instruments (strings, brass and woodwind) were taught in virtually all LEAs and that the majority also provided tuition in percussion, brass band and classical guitar. Recorder and piano were fairly widely taught, although there was some evidence that piano tuition was waning in favour of electronic instruments such as bass guitar, keyboards and synthesizer. About a quarter of LEAs taught voice and harp, and a small but substantial minority provided tuition in early instruments and a small range of Afro-Caribbean and Indian instruments.

These findings are compatible with an increased awareness in recent years of the need to broaden the music curriculum to embrace a range of periods, styles and cultures. Advances in microtechnology offer opportunities for children to generate a huge variety of different sounds which can be used in the composition and improvisation encouraged by the new GCSE syllabus. There has also been a growing consciousness of the need to break away from the Western tradition and to acquaint children with music from other cultures. There was some uncertainty, however, as to how this could be done through the instrumental service. While some senior staff fervently believed that children should have the opportunity to hear and try out instruments from different ethnic groups, others failed to see the need to introduce such instruments in their authority because their population was, in the words of one respondent, 'all-white Caucasian'. It is also important to remember that even where there was a very real desire to expand the range of instruments taught, the ability to do so was often severely limited by insufficient resources in terms of both the money to buy the instruments and the availability of specialists to teach them.

The main bulk of instrumental tuition was found to take place in the schools or to a lesser extent to be distributed between schools and music centres. By comparison, in a few authorities there were certain instruments, notably percussion, recorders and electric guitar, in which tuition was available only in the music centres.

Arrangements made for the purchase and allocation of instruments used for tuition were revealing. Sixty-eight per cent of LEAs provided most of the instruments in use from central funds supplemented by school capitations. Well over half of these authorities lent the instruments to children free of charge for an unlimited time and the rest either encouraged pupils to buy their own after a specified period or, more rarely, hired LEA stocks to them for a fee. At the other extreme were 28 per cent of authorities where most of the instruments were supplied by individual pupils. Although a few LEAs required children to provide their own instrument from the beginning, most allowed pupils a trial period in which to show a degree of progress and commitment.

The large majority of instrumental music services had their own budget allocations and a few were funded from the general music budget administered by the music adviser. In contrast, there were some instrumental services which received no direct financing and which had to compete with others in bids from general LEA funds. From 1984/5 to 1985/6, instrumental music allocations had been increased in 27 per cent of LEAs, many of them counties, and had been reduced in 18 per cent, largely the metropolitan districts.

Most authorities had spent money on the purchase of instruments and equipment, the maintenance and repair of instruments, and the purchase or hire of music for ensemble work. There are signs, however, of a fall-off in spending on instruments since 1983 and it must be remembered that on limited budgets it is difficult to replenish stocks let alone expand them or improve their quality. In most cases, budgets were clearly inadequate to meet costs and, despite a widespread belief that the service should be free for as many children as want it, most advisers and heads of service made requests for some kind of financial help from parents.

In 88 per cent of LEAs parents were asked to provide music for their child, and in 41 per cent they were asked for contributions towards at least one of the following: travel and subsistence for courses, tours and workshops; attendance at concerts; external examination fees and/or travel to examination centres; and sundries such as reeds, strings, shoulder pads and rosin. In 39 per cent of LEAs parents were asked to contribute to the maintenance and/or repair of instruments loaned to their child. The most 'freely' provided services were those in 19 authorities where most instruments were provided by the LEA, loaned free of charge for an unlimited period and where no maintenance or repair contribution was required. At the other extreme were five LEAs which not only requested a number of the contributions mentioned above but also asked parents for a regular 'voluntary contribution' towards their child's tuition.

5 Selection, Continuity and Progress

This chapter examines levels of LEA instrumental music provision across the country and considers how schools and pupils come to receive the service. Selection methods and criteria are described, and pupil 'drop-out' is discussed, with strategies for maximizing continuity of tuition. The monitoring of progress is then detailed in terms of records, reports, graded tests and examinations. Attention is paid to provision for children who are especially talented, and an account is given of the youth orchestras, bands and choirs which perform at home and abroad.

Level of provision

Pupils receiving instrumental tuition

Our survey sought information on the number of pupils receiving LEA instrumental music tuition in each authority. Eighty of the LEAs provided this information, although many of them were able to give approximations only. On the basis of these figures it is estimated that in the school year 1985/6 roughly 362,000 children in England and Wales were learning to play an instrument through LEA music services. As a proportion of the total school population (including infant schools, sixth form colleges and special schools) instrumental pupils accounted for some five to six per cent. In the LEAs, levels of provision ranged from two per cent at one extreme to 29 per cent (in a very small island authority) at the other. In most authorities, between three and eight per cent of school-age pupils were receiving tuition though, on average, the proportion tended to be highest in the London boroughs and Wales and lowest in the English counties. Overall these figures suggest that, despite local fluctuations due to economic cutbacks and falling rolls, the proportion across the country of schoolchildren learning to play an instrument has remained fairly stable in recent years. Precise figures are difficult to obtain, but in 1984 the HMI survey estimated the percentage to be between four and eight per cent and the Gulbenkian Report of 1978 put the figure at 'about five per cent' although it is not clear whether the latter included children learning privately.

Details of authorities with the highest and lowest proportion of pupils receiving instrumental tuition through the LEA service are given in Tables 5.1 and 5.2.

Table 5.1: *LEAs with highest percentage of pupils receiving instrumental music tuition (eight per cent or more)*

Type of LEA	Percentage of pupils learning	No. of pupils learning	Percentage of schools with tuition
Island	29	76	100
Island	11	800	100
London borough	11	2493	86
London borough	10	3062	76
Welsh	9	4831	not known
London borough	9	3200	not known
Metropolitan district	9	3240	83
Metropolitan district	8	2100	81
Metropolitan district	8	3807	84
Island	8	800	not known
London borough	8	2626	71
Welsh	8	4281	not known

The tables show that, in general, pupil coverage was positively related to school coverage: authorities with a relatively high percentage of instrumental pupils also made an input into a high proportion of their schools. With two exceptions, the same was true at the other end of the scale where authorities with the lowest percentage of instrumental pupils also covered a comparatively low proportion of their schools. However, as the tables indicate, one LEA made an input into 71 per cent of its schools and reached eight per cent of its pupils whereas another LEA covered 72 per cent of its schools and only reached two per cent of its pupil population. Thus, in the second case, a low level of provision was spread thinly to cover a relatively large number of schools. (The amount of instrumental teaching time available to different schools is discussed in Chapter 6, pp. 85–107.)

Table 5.2: *LEAs with lowest percentage of pupils receiving instrumental music tuition (three per cent or less)*

Type of LEA	Percentage of pupils learning	No. of pupils learning	Percentage of schools with tuition
English county	3	3000	37
English county	3	3500	65
English county	3	6035	30
English county	3	1500	28
English county	3	2586	43
Metropolitan district	3	1517	46
Metropolitan district	3	1100	48
Metropolitan district	2	1975	72

It is important to take the size of the authority into account. Table 5.1 shows that some of the smallest LEAs had the highest percentage of pupils learning to play an instrument. This was particularly true of the island authorities which had a small school population. It is also important to note that a similar number of pupils receiving tuition may represent a high level of provision in one authority and a low level in another. For example, the English counties which ranked among the lowest providers were in fact teaching as many pupils if not more than the highest providers. However, because the counties tended to be large, instrumental pupils represented only a small proportion of their school population.

The question arises as to how pupils come to receive LEA instrumental music tuition. With a relatively scarce resource such as this, some kind of selection would seem to be inevitable. However, since some schools do not have an input from the instrumental service for which pupils can be selected, this raises the question of how schools become recipients of the service in the first place. The selection of schools and pupils is discussed in detail below.

Schools with instrumental tuition

The questionnaire asked LEAs for details of the number of schools in their authority receiving regular visits from instrumental teaching staff. The figures revealed that the average LEA was providing instrumental tuition in about 65 per cent of its schools, and that on the whole the metropolitan districts and London boroughs were reaching a higher proportion of their schools than were the counties. Input varied considerably, ranging from 24 per cent of schools in one authority to 100 per cent in others. At the lower extreme was a county which had no music centres, which meant that all its instrumental tuition was concentrated in fewer than a quarter of its schools. At the other extreme were two authorities with instrumental input in all their schools. These were both very small authorities, one having special schools which also received tuition. Nine more LEAs covered all their schools except a few infant (or first) and special schools; all of these had music centres as well.

Primary and secondary schools

Given that various school systems are in operation across the country, the term 'primary' is used here to include infant, first, junior, infant and junior, middle deemed primary, and first and middle combined schools; and the term 'secondary' includes secondary, middle deemed secondary, and upper schools. The distribution of instrumental tuition between primary and secondary schools is shown in Table 5.3.

Table 5.3: *Distribution of instrumental music tuition in primary and secondary schools (94 LEAs)*

Schools with instrumental tuition	% LEAs
All or almost all secondary and some primary schools	74
All or almost all secondary and all or almost all primary schools	12
Some secondary and some primary schools	9
Primary schools only	1*
Not known	4
	100

* One LEA in which secondary school pupils received tuition in music centres only.

The table shows that by and large the secondary schools were more widely covered for instrumental tuition than the primaries. Altogether, 86 per cent of LEAs put instrumental teachers into all or almost all of their secondary schools. There are of course far more primary than secondary schools, and where instrumental staff are in short supply it is often considered more economical to allocate them to secondary schools and their main feeder primaries. None of the responding LEAs provided instrumental tuition exclusively to the secondary sector. One authority supplied instrumental staff only to primary schools; tuition for secondary pupils had been removed from the schools and was located entirely in the music centres.

Eleven LEAs provided instrumental tuition in all or almost all (i.e. 90 per cent or more) of their primary and secondary schools. Metropolitan districts in the north of England were particularly well-represented among these. Apart from one authority with nearly 300 schools, all the LEAs in this group were relatively small ranging in size from five to 115 schools.

By far the most widespread pattern, occurring in nearly three-quarters of the LEAs, was the provision of instrumental tuition in practically all secondary schools and some primaries. In the primary sector instrumental input was more likely to be found at the upper end of the age range; several respondents pointed out that all their junior but none of their infant departments were visited by instrumental teachers. Where middle school systems were in operation a similar pattern prevailed, with instrumental tuition being available to most of the upper and middle schools but only some, if any, of the first schools. On the other hand, at least four authorities started children on violin tuition in the nursery. At the other end of the age range most LEAs with sixth-form colleges included them in the instrumental scheme.

Special schools

More than a third (35) of the LEAs in our survey provided instrumental tuition in special schools, i.e. schools for children with special educational needs. One authority made an input into all of its (three) special schools; the rest provided tuition in selected schools.

Only eight authorities employed a member of staff with particular responsibility for instrumental tuition in special schools. Not all of these, however, had pupils who were learning to play a specialist instrument. What sometimes happened was that teachers with such responsibility were trying to bring general music education to children with special needs not only in special schools but also to those increasingly being integrated into mainstream classes or attending units attached to ordinary schools. Their work might include coordinating and supporting school-based music teachers and carrying out a certain amount of teaching in schools without music staff. Although they usually made use of instruments such as percussion, electric keyboards and guitars in their work, their involvement of specialist instrumental staff might extend as far as invitations to give demonstrations, concerts or workshops, thus giving children the opportunity to experience live music, though not necessarily with a view to learning to play an instrument.

Where consideration was being given to initiating instrumental tuition in special schools, the point was often made that such tuition would call for a particular kind of teacher who possessed certain qualities and skills. It was clear from our observations in both mainstream and special schools that the job demands infinite patience and understanding. It also requires a view of time and progress which is related to the individual child's capabilities. As one teacher explained: 'You have to know when to push the children and when not to in order to avoid frustrating them. It can take six months for some of them to play two notes.'

Some respondents foresaw organizational problems associated with introducing instrumental tuition in special schools. To assist anyone who might be contemplating such a move, here is an example of how one authority manages it. The LEA music team includes a coordinator for music in special education, a post which was created three years ago. The coordinator is based at the music centre from which the schools music service operates and is responsible for music in all eight of the authority's special schools and in units attached to mainstream schools. The work is carried out by a team of six: four peripatetic general music teachers, including the coordinator herself, who each visit two special schools for two or three days a week; one music therapist; and one instrumental brass teacher. The coordinator organizes her team on an integrated basis which is very flexible depending on the needs of children in the different schools: for example, a music teacher and the therapist together visit the pupils needing most help. The coordinator teaches three days a week at one school, working with all 70 of the pupils, and one day a week in another school. She regularly visits all the special schools and units and all members of her team. She arranges courses and workshops, and organizes fortnightly staff meetings after school with guest speakers. She also has a meeting once a fortnight with the music adviser and meets with other senior music staff twice a term.

The brass teacher visits five of the special schools, teaching a total of 79 pupils who are physically disabled or who have emotional and behavioural difficulties or moderate learning difficulties. She teaches the trumpet, cornet and baritone to children aged from nine to 16, writing most of their music for them. As part of their life skills course the older pupils travel by bus to the music centre where they take part in simple ensemble work.

How schools are selected

Since very few LEAs provide instrumental tuition in *every* school, the question arises as to how it is that some schools rather than others receive the service. Many authorities had a deliberate policy of priority for certain types of school, aiming to cover for example all secondary or upper and middle schools and to increase provision in primary schools. Those likely to be given least priority were infant or first schools, small rural schools and special schools.

One in five LEAs said that the distribution of their service was largely traditional: schools which had enjoyed provision in the past were likely to continue to do so and it could be difficult for other schools to gain access to a scarce resource. This caused concern to a number of advisers and heads of service who were anxious to distribute the service more equitably throughout their authority. Equity was particularly difficult to achieve without expanding the service because schools jealously guarded their existing provision and were reluctant to take the reduction in teaching hours which would be necessary for more schools to benefit. Several authorities reported that historical imbalances of provision, often dating back to the seventies, could not be rectified because of shortage of staff. Others warned that schools which were eligible through either policy or tradition were not unassailable and could have their existing input reduced or even withdrawn if they did not make good use of it; resources could then be redirected to schools requesting the service for the first time.

Nearly a third of LEAs expected schools with no instrumental tuition to take the initiative in requesting it. Even in authorities where the service sent out request forms, the onus was on the school to respond. Once a school had made a request a number of considerations were usually taken into account before a decision was made. The most frequently mentioned was the likelihood of support for music in the school. Support was judged in terms of whether the headteacher was interested and enthusiastic, whether there was a music specialist and whether there would be opportunities for children to practise their playing. Closely related to this was the ability of the school or pupils to 'use the service effectively'; provision might be discontinued if the new applicant was found to be squandering its input.

Another consideration, especially in rural areas, was the geographical location of the school and the availability of staff time to travel there. Rural schools might be selected only if parents could be relied upon to transport their children to the music centre for ensemble work; conversely, the fact that pupils were unable to reach a music centre for tuition could sometimes increase the chances of a school being chosen. Some of the counties favoured the major feeder primaries and schools which could function as area centres. In one authority, the designation of certain schools as area centres was the solution to the problem of coping with its small rural schools. Children were brought in to the centres not only for music but for other curricular activities such as drama and sport. This meant that scarce resources, including specialist teachers, were available to more children, and pupils from small schools were able to come together to form viable groups and teams.

The size of the school and the suitability of its facilities and accommodation were taken into account in some authorities. The availability of peripatetic staff also had to be considered. For example, a shortage of specialists in certain instruments affected the range of provision which could be made available to a school; double bass, percussion, oboe and bassoon were particularly mentioned in this respect. The range might also be affected by LEA policy. For example, it was common for strings not to be taught to beginners in the secondary school. This meant that children who attended primary schools with no string tuition were effectively denied the opportunity to learn such an instrument at school. On the other hand, good provision was likely to attract more: the cello, for example, might be introduced only in schools where upper strings had already proved to be successful. This raises the question of whether resources should be concentrated on 'successful' schools or whether they should be redistributed to cover all schools.

Regrettably, there were some authorities where no new requests could be considered. The service was unable to meet demand in terms of staff and teaching time, and resources were fully stretched in maintaining existing provision. Indeed, one adviser considered that shortages in his authority were so acute as to render the service elitist and this was in direct conflict with pressures to provide equal opportunities for all children. A senior instrumental teacher summed up the general feeling when he explained: 'Probably the most difficult task in organizing the (instrumental) scheme is the fair and equitable distribution of resources. A small increase in staffing would significantly ease this problem and engender the goodwill of parents, headteachers and governing bodies.'

Selection of pupils

Once a school has been granted an input from the instrumental music service the decision then has to be made as to which pupils should receive it. The survey showed that some form of selection operated everywhere, usually because resources simply could not meet demand. Although a few LEAs theoretically offered tuition to every child who wanted it, in practice a certain amount of selection took place either directly or indirectly in order to pick up 'the children who were most likely to benefit'.

Who selects?

The task of deciding which pupils should receive tuition rested with different people depending on the authority. In two-thirds of LEAs the decision was made jointly between the instrumental service and the schools, although it was not always clear who had the final say. Most commonly, selection was made by the instrumental teacher in close consultation with the headteacher and music specialist or class teacher as appropriate. A few also involved the parents in their deliberations. In a further one-quarter of LEAs the final decision rested with the instrumental service, usually after discussions with school staff and parents. The decision was made by the music adviser or senior staff in some authorities but in most LEAs it was made by the instrumental teacher. In the remaining authorities selection was ultimately in the hands of the schools. The choice rested with the headteacher, music teacher or head of music and was sometimes made after screening by the instrumental service or consultation with parents and tutors.

LEA guidelines on selection

About three in five LEAs provided guidelines for those responsible for the selection of pupils. The rest left the matter to the discretion of the people concerned although verbal guidance might be available from senior instrumental staff if required. Selection in these latter authorities occasionally formed the topic for discussion at INSET meetings and at least two of them were in the process of preparing guidelines. There was a reluctance among some senior staff to be seen to prescribe 'hard and fast rules' and in one authority an attempt to offer guidelines to schools had been rejected by the headteachers.

Guidelines varied from those which dealt solely with administrative matters to those which offered step-by-step instructions on the whole process. Administrative guidance related to such matters as the best time for a child to start (preferably the autumn or spring terms rather than the summer which was likely to contain too many interruptions), arrangements for the use of an instrument and a reminder to obtain formal agreement from the pupil's parents. Step-by-step instructions usually began with the child expressing an interest and covered the various characteristics considered to be desirable in the pupil. Here is an example of the guidelines offered in an authority where selection was made jointly by the instrumental service and the schools.

Example of guidelines on selection in one LEA

Selection of pupils for instrumental tuition

All schools will have their own detailed method of selection of pupils suitable for instrumental tuition. However, the following points should be borne in mind when making such selection:

(a) Pupils who have expressed an interest in learning an instrument should be given a copy of the relevant information to take home to discuss with their parents.

(b) Pupils who do show an interest should be seen by the appropriate instrumental teacher to check physical suitability – coordination, dental problems (wind and brass) etc. – although enthusiasm may sometimes surmount these problems.

It is vital that the school assesses as accurately as possible the home support and backing which a pupil is likely to receive. It is strongly recommended that, whenever possible, the Headteacher or Head of Department should meet parents and explain their responsibilities. This is likely to ensure a seriousness of purpose and at least give a chance of eventual success.

(c) Some tests of musical potential should be given either by the instrumental teacher or by the class music teacher as appropriate.

(d) Starting age. This needs to be discussed with the instrumental teacher as this will vary according to the instrument.

(e) Musical experience and aptitude. The pupils should have shown interest and demonstrated aptitude in class music lessons as appropriate to their age and opportunities. A great deal of time is saved if the pupil is familiar with elementary musical notation and is able either to play a recorder or to sing reasonably well in tune. A pupil's commitment and level of concentration might also be taken into account. These are not absolute requirements and discretion must be exercised.

(f) Choice of instrument. The brochure entitled 'So you want to play an instrument' outlines in some detail many of the problems and pitfalls which are often encountered in learning a musical instrument. Since for the most part children will be too young to take account of such facts when choosing an instrument, suitable advice from the teacher is of great importance. Eventually, pupils will be expected to purchase their own instruments. The cost of instruments therefore should be borne in mind when the initial choice of instrument is made.

In this example, the actual details of the method of selection are left to the individuals concerned and guidance is given on the main points to be borne in mind. It is interesting to note how various people are drawn into the selection process. It is the school's responsibility to follow up the child's initial expression of interest by providing information to take home. The school also has the task of assessing parental support and explaining to parents what their responsibilities will be. Parents are involved at an early stage and their role is considered vital to their child's success. The class teacher and instrumental teacher each have a part to play in determining the child's suitability.

Most of the points in the example are concerned with the factors which are considered to be important when assessing suitability: enthusiasm, physical problems, parental support, musical potential, age, musical experience and aptitude, commitment and concentration. Our survey showed that similar factors were taken into account in many authorities. These are discussed in more detail below.

Considerations when selecting pupils

The questionnaire asked respondents about considerations which should be taken into account when selecting pupils for instrumental tuition. The results are presented in Table 5.4.

Almost all respondents considered at least four of the points shown in Table 5.4 to be important, and a third of them believed all eight should be taken into account. Those which were considered important by almost all respondents were: the pupil's enthusiasm, evidence of musical ability, physical suitability and evidence of commitment.

(a) Enthusiasm and evidence of commitment
Enthusiasm was an almost universal consideration and was deemed by some to supersede all else. Others considered that evidence of commitment was paramount and looked for indicators of the child's 'stickability' or perseverance with other school activities and interests.

Table 5.4: *Considerations to be taken into account when selecting pupils for instrumental music tuition (94 LEAs)*

Considerations	% LEAs
Enthusiasm	98
Evidence of musical ability	94
Physical suitability	93
Evidence of commitment	92
Musical potential as measured by aural tests	84
Parental support	82
Age	68
Academic ability	41
Other	12

In a study of peripatetic teachers' selection procedures, Cooper (1985) warns that the child's enthusiasm and interest, considered in his survey to be the most important factor, need to be approached with care since they may fade as the novelty wears off. Our own study showed that in many LEAs beginners take up instrumental tuition for a trial period of several weeks, a term or a year, thus allowing time to assess whether enthusiasm and commitment are likely to last.

(b) Evidence of musical ability
Evidence of musical ability was taken here to mean, for example, that the child was able to sing or was already playing the recorder. Responses indicated that this was the second most widespread consideration when selecting beginners. It might also be taken into account in relation to certain instruments. For example, it was not uncommon for tuition in the bassoon to be offered to pupils who had already reached a certain level of proficiency in the oboe or clarinet.

(c) Physical suitability
Physical suitability was said to be especially important in relation to certain instruments; for example embouchure for brass, coordination and dexterity for strings, and the size and stretch of the fingers for woodwind. Clearly these factors need to be treated with discretion. Whilst acknowledging that certain physical characteristics appear to assist progress on various instruments, Mills (1985) argues that 'we know of no physical characteristic of normal healthy people which implies that they do not have an unusual potential for specific instruments' and that a child who passionately wants to play should be allowed to do so despite poor coordination, small hands or narrow

finger-tips. Some respondents in our study referred to the importance of the child's choosing 'the right instrument' and one authority's own survey on selection found that instrumental suitability was rated by teachers as highest in importance.

Two further factors were widely held to be important: musical potential as measured by aural tests, and parental support.

(d) Musical potential

The measurement of musical potential by aural tests was widely favoured in principle, but clearly aroused strong feelings as to which aural tests should be used. Although several LEAs indicated that they used Bentley tests in the selection of pupils, others expressly pointed out that their tests were of an informal nature and were often devised by the instrumental teachers concerned. Bentley tests, described in Bentley's *Measures of Musical Abilities* (Bentley, 1966), consist of a battery of tests which attempt to measure four aspects of musical ability: pitch discrimination, tonal memory, rhythmic memory and chord analysis. Despite the fact that Bentley himself did not advocate that the results should be used to select pupils, the tests have been found to be widely used for this purpose (Barnes, 1982, Cooper, 1985). Our survey revealed that some authorities were recommending the tests to be used selectively. One authority, for example, advocated that the Bentley tests should be given to every prospective pupil as part of the selection process but that the questions on chords should be left out. Another LEA pointed to the usefulness of Bentley's pitch discrimination test but stressed that the testing should be only one of the factors taken into account when selecting pupils. New tests which are expected to be useful in selecting pupils for instrumental tuition have recently been devised for use with children aged seven to 14. The tests are concerned with the abilities to perceive small differences in pitch and to maintain a steady pulse (Mills, 1988).

Although many instrumental teachers devise their own simple tests, some said they believed that aural tests of any kind should be treated with caution because they are not always predictors of musical potential: some children who do badly on aural tests prove later to be good players. This point has been made by Evans (1985) who argues that some kind of continuous assessment over a period of time might be useful in predicting musical potential, especially as 'the most intangible yet potent aspect of musical capacity – that of aesthetic response – would seem to defy measurement entirely'. In some LEAs, particularly where it was believed that all children who wanted to learn should have the opportunity to try, no tests of any kind were used at the selection stage. Again, a trial period was seen to be advantageous during which, as one adviser wrote to parents, 'we will discover whether your child has the necessary physical and aural coordination and shows willingness to persist in a difficult undertaking'.

(e) Parental support

Although parental support was widely held to be a worthy consideration, opinion varied as to its importance when selecting pupils. One respondent pointed out that, while parental support was desirable, a child would not be barred from learning to play an instrument if the support were not forthcoming. From the material enclosed with many of the questionnaires it was apparent that other respondents felt differently. The support or involvement of parents was said to be essential, even vital, for the pupil's success. Some went so far as to state in their notes to parents and staff that 'parents must declare their support before a child can be considered for inclusion in the instrumental scheme', and forms were provided for this purpose.

There was a general feeling that parents of intending instrumentalists should be fully aware of their role and responsibilities before tuition began, and parents were usually asked to sign their agreement. An outline of what is involved when a child learns to play an instrument was sent to parents in the form of a letter or booklet. The parents' responsibilities with regard to the safeguarding of LEA-owned instruments were explained including, where applicable, arrangements for instrumental maintenance, hire or purchase. Support was sought mainly in providing regular opportunities and suitable facilities for practice, and in encouraging the child to participate in ensembles at school and music centre. The rather more difficult task of maintaining the pupil's morale when the novelty wore off was particularly well-described in the following example:

> Above all try to encourage your child and take a lively interest in how he or she is progressing. Ask about the lessons. Look at the books being used and observe any comments made by the teacher. Do encourage your child to practise daily, though it is a good idea not to nag or be too harsh as this will do no real good and only cause tension and unhappiness. Fostering interest through encouragement is by far the best method. Also do be pleased, and say so, if obvious progress is being made and if perhaps a piece is played rather well.'

(f) Age

Two-thirds of respondents considered that a pupil's age should be taken into account at selection. There were obvious age limitations imposed by the size of certain instruments; others, notably strings, could be scaled down in size and could therefore be made available to younger players. Apart from this, starting-age was sometimes dictated by the LEA's policy for instrumental tuition. For example, where provision was mainly focused on the secondary sector most children were unable to begin before the age of 11 which is considered late for some instruments. On the other hand, while many LEAs were increasingly providing tuition in primary schools this could have the effect of closing the gate on would-be beginners in the secondary school, especially with regard to strings. Recognizing this dilemma, some authorities provided opportunities for pupils to begin at any age within reason provided resources were available. Evidence of this practice was seen in action in LEAs where ensembles were constituted according to ability rather than age and where, for example, pupils aged from nine to 17 were playing alongside each other in groups ranging from the beginners' brass band to the area youth orchestra.

Our questionnaire sought information on the approximate age at which most pupils began tuition on the various instruments. The findings are presented in Table 5.5.

The table shows which instruments were usually begun at primary school and which were left till the secondary stage as well as those which spanned these age groups. The instruments can be grouped into those which are begun mainly at the following stages: lower primary, upper primary, upper primary and lower secondary, lower secondary, and lower and upper secondary.

(i)   Lower primary

Instruments usually started in the infant or first and lower junior school: recorders, violin and cello. Violins and cellos were scaled-down to a quarter, an eighth and even a sixteenth in size for young players. From the table it is clear that the violin is regarded as an instrument to be taken up early; none of the LEAs in our survey made a general practice of introducing the violin in the secondary school. In some authorities it was possible for children to begin violin tuition in the nursery, especially where the Suzuki method was used.

(ii)   Upper primary

Instruments usually started in the junior and lower middle school: harp, viola, flute, clarinet, trumpet, brass band, piano, harmonium, tabla, sitar, double bass, horn and trombone. With all these instruments there were a few authorities where tuition was introduced in the infant school and others where it could be started at secondary age. The strings again had the advantage of being able to be scaled down in size: for example, double basses of half and quarter size were

Table 5.5: Age at which most pupils began an instrument (94 LEAs)

Instrument	Age in majority of LEAs	(Range across all providing LEAs)
recorders	6–8	(5–11)
violin	7–8	(3–9)
cello	7–9	(6–11)
harp	8–10	(7–12)
viola	8–11	(6–13)
flute	8–11	(6–12)
clarinet	8–11	(6–12)
trumpet	8–11	(7–12)
brass band	8–11	(7–13)
piano	8–11	(5–14)
percussion	8–11	(7–13)
classical guitar	8–9,11	(7–12)
steel band	8–9,11	(7–12)
early instruments	8–12	(7–14)
harmonium	9	(7–13)
tabla	9–10	(7–13)
sitar	9–11	(7–13)
double bass	9–11	(7–13)
oboe	9–11	(7–13)
horn	9–11	(7–13)
trombone	9–11	(7–12)
bassoon	9–12	(7–13)
tuba	9–12	(8–15)
synthesizer/keyboards	11	(8–14)
electric/bass guitar	11–12	(8–15)
saxophone	11–13	(8–14)
voice	11–13,16	(5–16)

becoming increasingly popular since their promotion in the Yorke Mini-Bass Project for teaching double bass to younger pupils. A variety of wind and brass instruments were widely introduced in the upper primary school. Flute and clarinet beginners were often, though not always, children who had achieved some proficiency on the recorder. Both the trumpet and brass band instruments were most likely to be started at the age of nine, and Asian instruments, though of very limited availability, were also more likely to be introduced at this stage. The greatest age range was spanned by beginners of the piano, with tuition commencing from five to 14 across the country.

(iii) Upper primary and lower secondary
Instruments usually started in the junior, middle or lower secondary school: percussion, classical guitar, steel band, oboe, bassoon, tuba and early instruments other than the recorder. Classical guitar and steel band were most likely to be introduced at one of two stages: either at eight to nine or on transfer to secondary school. Percussion was also widely begun at the ages of nine and 11, and the first year of the secondary school was a peak time for starting oboe, bassoon and tuba. Early instruments, where available, were introduced at various stages.

(iv) Lower secondary
Instruments usually started in the early years of secondary school or at the upper end of the middle school: synthesizer, keyboards, electric guitar, bass guitar and saxophone. All of these were particularly likely to start at the age of 11.

(v) Lower and upper secondary
The only 'instrument' in this group was the voice. It was unique in that tuition was usually begun either in the early secondary and upper middle school years or at the age of 16; no other instrument was generally begun at 16. It was widely held that formal tuition should not begin until the voice had matured, although pupils often had the opportunity to begin choral singing earlier. Singing was believed to provide a good basis for instrumental work and there were opportunities in one or two LEAs for children to join singing groups from the age of five.

(g) Academic ability
Academic ability received the lowest poll in our list of considerations at selection, although as many as 41 per cent of respondents said it should be taken into account. However, some of these added that they believed it to be the least important consideration. Interviews with school and instrumental staff revealed that opinions on the merits of academic ability were divided. While some considered, for example, that the ability to read and retain information was advantageous for instrumental tuition, others argued that learning to play an instrument could give the academically unsuccessful child the chance to succeed.

The relationship between musical ability and general ability has been addressed in a number of studies on selection but conclusions have been tentative. For example, Mawbey (1973) noted that as far as secondary pupils were concerned verbal reasoning scores had little bearing on whether children continued with instrumental tuition or not, whereas in the case of primary pupils there was some relationship between perseverance with instrumental lessons and reading age or verbal reasoning scores. On the other hand, the UK Council for Music Education and Training (UKCMET) make it quite clear in their document on Musical Giftedness in the Primary School (UKCMET, 1982) that the musically gifted child should not be confused with the highly intelligent child: 'we are not considering music for gifted children (i.e. children termed as gifted because they have a high intellect) but children whose gifts are specifically musical' (p.3).

(h) Other considerations
Besides those already discussed, some respondents added other considerations which they believed to be important at selection. These included the child's personal qualities such as alertness, independence and self-discipline, school support particularly in terms of the provision and supervision of practice facilities, and evidence of sibling success.

Hidden selection

Apart from the explicit considerations and criteria described above, there are of course many other factors which interact during the selection process and which effectively put instrumental tuition beyond the reach of certain children. This kind of 'hidden' selection can operate even in LEAs which profess a policy of open access to all who want it. Assuming that a school has instrumental tuition, there are general factors such as the need for low pupil:teacher ratios in instrumental teaching which means that only a small proportion of pupils in the school can have lessons. There are also the various costs entailed which, however small, may preclude children whose parents are not sufficiently disadvantaged to entitle them to special concessions but who nonetheless feel they cannot afford to contribute. The choice of instrument to be learned may be restricted by the fact that the parents do not have a car in which to help the child transport it to and fro.

Apart from general factors of this kind there are more specific ones associated with the people making the selection. While certain criteria or considerations may be recommended by the music adviser or head of service, the actual task of selection is usually carried out by other members of staff who have their own personal views and priorities which can influence selection. For example, in an LEA with a policy of open access and the free loan of instruments, one primary headteacher said that in her school catchment area there were homes to which she could not allow a musical instrument to be taken. In her view it was important that players practise at home and she would therefore not include children from such homes in the group presented to the instrumental teacher for selection. The opposite view was expressed by another primary head who adopted a deliberate policy of positive discrimination by including socially disadvantaged children in the group presented to the instrumental teacher.

Instrumental teachers also hold views which may influence selection. One declared that he should not have to waste his very limited time in a school on a child who was difficult and disruptive. Another welcomed 'difficult' children in the belief that in a small-group situation he could build up a relationship with the pupil which it was impossible for a class teacher to achieve.

The selection process

Interviews with school and instrumental staff revealed that actual procedures for selection varied from school to school even where guidance was given by the authority. The first step in identifying potential instrumental pupils was usually taken by the school, a group of children being presented to the instrumental teacher by the head, class teacher or music specialist. At this stage the children were identified either by the fact that they had 'expressed an interest', perhaps arising from a concert or demonstration given by a visiting group of players (staff and/or older pupils); or because they were considered to have some musical aptitude as demonstrated by, for example, their ability to read music or play the recorder. The number of children selected at this stage might be dictated by the number of places or instruments available. Some class teachers said they would only choose children who were well-behaved or who were sufficiently able in their class work not to fall behind when missing time to attend instrumental lessons. In secondary schools it was not uncommon for heads of music to administer the Bentley tests to prospective candidates before presenting them for tuition.

Once the instrumental teacher is faced with a group of potential players, the next stage in the selection process takes place. This varies in rigour: some teachers accept, at least for a trial period, all children who want to learn. Others adopt their own selection procedures in the belief that limited resources should be directed at those most likely to benefit; in our case studies these included administering a simple aural test, and talking with pupils to assess the extent of their interest and likely commitment. Some teachers gave priority to children who could already read music. This stage was followed by contact with the parents and a trial period of tuition.

The importance of choosing the 'right' instrument was emphasized by some teachers who, as far as possible, provided opportunities for aspiring players to blow, pluck or strum so that personal preferences and physical size and suitability could be taken into consideration. Indeed, Ben-Tovim and Boyd (1987) argue that the principal reason for drop-out in the early days is that children set out to learn an instrument which does not suit them physically, mentally or emotionally, and that choosing 'the wrong instrument can and does put children off music for life'.

It was believed that no method of selection was foolproof and it was generally accepted as inevitable that some pupils would discontinue tuition at an early stage. Some teachers deliberately started with inflated groups to allow for what they called 'natural wastage'.

Pupil progress

Continuity of tuition

Most instrumental teachers expected some pupils to discontinue when their initial interest had waned after the first few weeks. The next point at which children were likely to give up was when the work became technically more difficult, such as when moving on to the upper register in clarinet-playing. Once this point was passed, pupils were likely to continue at least until transfer from primary to secondary or from middle to upper school. It was generally acknowledged that children were more likely to give up tuition at transfer than at any other stage in their school career. Once they reached adolescence, however, they faced increasing pressures on their time from homework and examinations, especially in what were considered to be the more 'academic' subjects. Parents who were anxious that their children should not miss lessons in these subjects sometimes encouraged pupils to give up instrumental tuition in order to concentrate on work which they, the parents, considered to be more important. However, instances were cited of parents who surmounted this problem by paying for their child to continue music tuition from a private teacher out of school hours.

Adolescence was also a time when pupils were under pressure to participate in a wide variety of activities, and music was likely to be in competition with new diversions and experiences. In the third year of the secondary school children selected their options; if music was not one of them, instrumental tuition might be abandoned either then or with the approach of GCSE and 'A' level exams. There were also points during the instrumental pupil's progression at which cessation was likely to occur: Grades 3 and 5 were notable examples.

As well as these obvious hurdles in the child's career, there are also more general factors which can operate at any stage. Teachers referred in particular to the pressure of the peer group who may regard instrumentalists as 'sissies'. They also mentioned the discouraging effects of poor tuition, inadequate parental and school support, and the child's own inability to advance beyond a personal plateau of achievement. It was generally acknowledged that a period of prolonged absence from school could irreparably damage a pupil's progress. It was also true that socio-economic factors played a part; for example, in some areas it had been noted that cessation increased with a rise in unemployment.

Several advisers and senior instrumental staff pointed out that one of the major reasons why children give up is that they are often introduced to instrumental tuition before they are ready. Staff considered that 'readiness' should be fostered through the primary music curriculum and that singing could provide an important start. As one adviser said, 'if instrumental teachers are faced with teaching a sense of rhythm and pitch, aural awareness and the reading of notation along with the technical complexities of the instrument in one half hour lesson per week, is it surprising that many (pupils) give up?'

Attitudes to pupils giving up tuition varied from teacher to teacher. Some considered that more rigour in selection would ensure that only pupils who were likely to continue would be given the opportunity to learn. Others believed that any musical experience, however brief, could not be regarded as a waste. It was widely acknowledged that some children wanted to give up because they had chosen the wrong instrument and, recognizing this, teachers sometimes allowed another instrument to be tried. However, in many cases limited resources dictated that there could be no second chance.

Asked whether they would ever encourage a child to discontinue tuition, teachers expressed a range of opinions. Many agreed that as long as children wanted to learn they should be allowed to do so; indeed some felt they had no right to ask a child to discontinue. The emphasis was on enjoyment, and less able players should not be deprived of the pleasure of learning an instrument. As one teacher said: 'I am under no pressure to produce genius, I simply want to see as many children as possible enjoy their playing.' Others disagreed, asserting that 'progress is enjoyment' and pupils who do not advance with the rest will not enjoy the experience. The first group said they would only advise children to give up if they had lost interest and were making absolutely no effort at all, although the initiative in such cases usually came from the pupils. Where progress was slow, they (the teachers) would persevere in the belief that playing an instrument could fulfil a social or personal need in the child. The more demanding teachers said they expected pupils to work hard and they would ask children to discontinue if they were wasting places which others might want. They considered that pupils who were 'getting nowhere' or who were 'holding back the group' should be persuaded to withdraw so that attention could be concentrated on the rest. It should also be noted here that in some authorities tuition was conditional on the pupil's joining an ensemble; failure to do so could mean that tuition had to be withdrawn.

Once it was agreed that a pupil should discontinue, the process of 'de-selection' was put into operation. In many cases this consisted simply of informing the parents, head and classteacher concerned. Some LEAs had very clear procedures for de-selection. Examples made available to us showed that these procedures usually involved close consultation between school and instrumental staff and formal letters to parents. Some began with a warning to parents which was followed up later if matters did not improve. Similarly, where de-selection was instigated by the child, a back-up letter from the parents was usually required. Once de-selection had taken place, the fact was noted on the pupil's record card.

The formality of these procedures suggests that de-selection was something to be avoided if at all possible and continuity encouraged. In our case-study authorities deliberate attempts were made to nurture pupils through the stages at which they were most likely to give up. At LEA level the main target was transfer from the primary to the secondary sector. Three of the four LEAs tried to ensure that, wherever possible, children who had begun tuition in the primary school had the same instrumental teacher after transfer. This proved impossible where the existence of grammar and independent schools, coupled with wider parental choice, meant that pupils could transfer to schools well beyond the area covered by their instrumental teacher. Other LEA strategies for continuity on transfer included the passing on of pupil records, the loan of unused secondary school instruments to older primary children, and a link scheme whereby heads of music from secondary schools taught music in their feeder primaries in order to establish a relationship with future pupils.

Teachers also had strategies for encouraging continuity. They pointed out that one of the advantages of starting instrumental tuition in the primary school was that commitment was likely to be assured before the time of transfer. When pupils showed signs of giving up, teachers usually tried to encourage them 'over the hump'. In fact, some older pupils told us that they would have given up long ago if it had not been for a timely word of support from a teacher. One enthusiastic 15 year-old brass player explained that 'after about six or seven weeks you feel like dropping out, but once you have passed this stage it's OK'. Another said, 'I got fed up around the second to third year but Mr. G (head of music in the school) had a word with me and I carried on'. She added that she was glad she had 'stuck at it because now it's so rewarding'. Flagging interest was also said to be revived by opportunities to take part in ensemble work. Both the pupils quoted above played in local brass bands and expected to continue to do so after leaving school.

The demands of the secondary school curriculum meant that class-based teachers were often disapproving of pupils who left their lessons for instrumental tuition and some children succumbed in the face of conflicting pressures. In an attempt to minimize this, instrumental lessons were usually rotated across the timetable so that players did not miss the same subject too often. The need to take time to study for 16 plus examinations was recognized by some teachers who allowed their pupils a term's break from instrumental tuition around that time.

Interviews with instrumental teachers revealed that in most cases they were teaching a predominance of girls. Teachers reported that more girls came forward for selection and fewer girls gave up. This was especially true of woodwind where as many as 80 and 90 per cent of the pupils taught by individual teachers were female. Three out of four strings teachers reported a preponderance of girls, whereas half the brass teachers had either an even balance or a majority of boys. At primary age, when most strings players begin, girls were said to be better coordinated physically than boys. Teachers of various instruments agreed that girls were more receptive at the start, inclined to work harder and likely to progress more quickly. Boys, on the other hand, were considered to be less mature, took their playing less seriously and were more easily discouraged or distracted. The attitude of the school towards boy instrumentalists was believed to be very important: although some headteachers encouraged boys to concentrate their energies on sport rather than music, others, recognizing that boys are afraid of appearing to be 'sissies', attempted by their own enthusiasm to foster a more positive image of music. However, the general feeling among the teachers was that when boys persevered with their instrumental tuition they usually made really good players.

Records and reports

Asked for details of any system they might have for recording children's progress in instrumental music, about one in three LEAs referred to records which were kept on each pupil, usually in the form of a record card, sheet or book where relevant information was regularly entered by the instrumental teacher. Information varied from a simple record of attendances made, examinations taken and ensembles joined to continuous assessments based on marks for attitude, effort, attainment and so on. In some cases records were also held centrally and/or at the music centres. A few LEAs had instituted profiling systems; this type of information was sometimes held by the school where it formed part of the pupil's general music profile. An instrumental music profile might contain information on, for instance, the pupil's musical ability, potential, motivation, diligence and parental support as well as work covered and examinations taken.

Some LEAs emphasized the importance of regular practice stating that the authority reserved the right to discontinue tuition 'if pupils fail to do the required amount of practice'. It was the responsibility of either the service or the schools to implement this policy. *Music from 5 to 16* (GB. DES,1985d) laid this responsibility firmly in the lap of the schools by recommending that a teacher should be designated in the school to 'ensure that pupils carry out regular practice between lessons and arrange for it to be supervised wherever appropriate' (p.22). Several advisers made the point that instrumental music must be shown to be as important as any other school work undertaken by the child and to this end they had devised visible systems for rewarding regular practice, notably by awarding badges for continuous effort in this direction.

Attitudes towards formal record-keeping varied, some advisers pointing out that they were anxious not to make rules and relied instead on the professionalism and goodwill of their staff. In many cases instrumental teachers devised their own record systems, especially with regard to practice. Pupils were encouraged to keep diaries or charts on which they recorded practice done at home and these were signed by the parents. The practice record served as an incentive for the pupil and as an indicator if interest waned. Some teachers offered rewards such as weekly gold stars and end-of-term prizes for sustained efforts. By no means all teachers kept records of practice or progress. Some had tried and given up because pupils forgot to make a note of their practising or forged their parents' signatures. Others considered that the tutor books used by their pupils provided an adequate record of progress and perseverance, particularly if the date was noted when each piece was mastered. As one teacher commented: 'Children make progress when they are pleased and proud about what they have done.'

Nearly half the authorities in our survey said they provided written reports to parents on progress in instrumental music. They were usually completed by the instrumental teacher and sent to parents either directly or through the schools; in some cases headteachers or music specialists in the schools had the opportunity to add their comments. Copies of the reports might be held by the schools and the music centres. One LEA issued an instrumental report 'book' on each pupil which was used throughout the child's school career. A few provided formal opportunities at the music centres for parents to meet instrumental staff to discuss their child's progress.

Provision for exceptionally talented pupils

Although a precise definition of musical giftedness is not easy to obtain, educationists have been unanimous in pointing out that children with special talent should be identified at as early a stage as possible. The UKCMET (1982) booklet *Musical Giftedness in the Primary School* points out that 'more often than not this identification will have to be made in our schools' (p.1). The vast majority of LEAs (88 per cent of those in our survey) made some kind of special provision, albeit in some cases only rarely, for children who were considered to be exceptionally talented in music. The most common forms of provision are shown in Table 5.6.

Table 5.6: *Provision for exceptionally talented pupils (94 LEAs)*

Type of provision	% LEAs
Travel expenses	54
Assisted places at specialist music schools	48
Bursaries, awards or own scheme for private individual tuition	47
Assisted attendance at junior department of conservatoire	41
Other (e.g. assisted purchase of instrument, course fees, exam fees, scholarships)	34

More than half the authorities provided assisted travel for talented pupils to attend master classes, specialist music lessons, concerts, auditions and so on. Almost a half offered financial support to children attending specialist music schools, although amounts varied between authorities. Specialist music schools such as the Purcell, Chetham's, the

Yehudi Menuhin, and Wells Cathedral School aim to provide a balanced education for 'musically gifted' children, many of whom go on to careers in music. Pupils are admitted by audition and either are supported entirely by their parents or receive assistance from bursaries and trusts, government grants or LEA support.

Almost as many LEAs offered bursaries and awards or ran their own scheme enabling especially talented pupils to receive private individual tuition. A substantial number of authorities gave assistance to children attending the junior departments of conservatoires or music colleges. These children, normally aged ten to 18, attend the colleges on Saturday mornings throughout term time. Individual tuition is given on a principal instrument and in some cases on a second and third instrument as well. There is class tuition in theory and musicianship, and opportunities to take part in ensembles, orchestras and choirs. LEA support varies considerably: at the junior department of one London college in 1985, for example, 161 places out of a total of 280 were supported entirely or in part by 19 authorities who were currently sponsoring from one to 37 pupils each. It must be remembered, however, that some LEAs are not within reasonable travelling distance of a music college, even if they consider such support to be desirable.

A third of authorities made other forms of provision for exceptional pupils. These included the purchase or assisted purchase of certain instruments; assistance with course fees and tours with prestigious groups; scholarship schemes; support for cathedral choristerships; annual bursaries to be spent at the pupils' discretion on instruments, courses or private tuition; the payment of advanced examination and audition fees; and assistance in cases of hardship. A few LEAs had local trust funds or bequests on which to draw, and a small number (six) had their own music schools for especially talented young musicians in their authority.

Graded tests and examinations

Asked whether their authority encouraged instrumental pupils to take external graded examinations (e.g. the examinations of the Associated Board of the Royal Schools of Music), the majority (83 per cent) of respondents said they did. A further ten per cent pointed out that it was not the policy of their authority to either encourage or discourage children from taking such exams since the decision was left to individual pupils and their teachers and parents. It was usual for parents to pay the examination fee and sometimes also to pay for an accompanist if required. Some authorities were willing to pay fees at least for Associated Board examinations, although candidates wishing to enter for examinations conducted by other boards might have to make other arrangements.

Nearly one third of the LEAs had devised their own graded tests for instrumental pupils who were, of course, at liberty also to take external examinations if they wished to do so. Local tests varied in level from one authority to another; some LEAs were still in the process of developing tests for the different instrumental groups. Authorities ranged from those who had instituted simple preliminary tests and exams up to the equivalent of Associated Board Grade 3, to those who had constructed five or six local grades. The advantages of these tests were that entry was free and that children could experience a measure of 'success' from the start. They were also a useful means of monitoring progress and structuring record-keeping. Several authorities were planning to initiate such a scheme.

Ensembles, bands, orchestras and choirs

All authorities provided opportunities for instrumental pupils to participate in formal group activities of some kind: ensembles, bands, orchestras, choirs. In many cases the groups were graded in difficulty so that children could proceed by audition through a structured system from beginner level to the more prestigious county or borough groups. Such a system could function as a record of the pupil's progress. In some authorities pupils from independent schools and children receiving private instrumental tuition were also eligible to participate in these groups.

The vast majority of LEAs (93 per cent) had youth ensembles (orchestras, bands or choirs) at county or borough level. The county youth orchestra, for example, often represented the top of a pyramid of groups through which children progressed, usually with keen competition for places. LEAs were more likely to have youth orches-tras and bands than choirs (Table 5.7). The counties were particularly well-represented in this respect. Some of the larger authorities had more than one county or borough orchestra and several also had a youth jazz orchestra. County or borough bands were of many kinds including brass, concert, dance, jazz, percussion and steel. A few authorities also had other groups at this level including guitar, recorder and early music ensembles. County or borough youth choirs were less common, but a few LEAs also had opera groups or choirs consisting of pupils, staff and parents.

Table 5.7: *Number of LEAs with county or borough youth ensembles (94 LEAs)*

Type of ensemble	% LEAs
Orchestras	93
Bands	80
Choirs	29
None of these	7

Seven of the smaller authorities had no groups at borough level but they all offered opportunities for ensemble work in local areas. More than three-quarters of the LEAs had area orchestras, bands or choirs, often based at or organized by the music centres (also see Chapter 7, pp. 108–41). Some offered a very wide range of opportunities at this level: one authority, for example, had 32 local groups for instrumental and choral work, quite apart from school-based groups. It was usual for children to progress through local groups to the county or borough groups, and there were sometimes opportunities for them to continue taking part after leaving school. Programmes from public performances by the various groups revealed a wide range of music. Always in evidence were works by western classical and modern composers. Many performances also included traditional folk tunes, excerpts from modern musicals, jazz, pop, film and television themes and new compositions. Occasionally music was performed in combination with drama or poetry.

Instrumental groups or choirs from almost all (94 per cent) of the LEAs in our survey had given performances outside their own authority. Groups had taken part in courses, competitions and concerts, had performed at prestigious venues such as the Royal Albert Hall and the Royal Festival Hall in London and St. David's Hall, Cardiff, and had participated in major events such as the National Festival of Music for Youth and the Edinburgh Festival. Many groups had toured abroad or taken part in regular visits and exchanges. The range of countries visited by the various groups was enormous and included most of Europe, Canada and the United States, Brazil, Hong Kong, Australia and the USSR. In this way the instrumental music service functions as a major national and international asset, providing an important vehicle for cultural exchange.

Summary

It is estimated that in 1985/6 some 362,000 children in England and Wales were receiving tuition through the instrumental music service.

Most services were reaching between three and eight per cent of their school population. Although precise figures are difficult to obtain, it would appear that in spite of serious reductions in some authorities, the overall proportion of school children receiving tuition has remained fairly constant in recent years.

Since there are very few authorities which provide the service to all their schools, opportunities for children to receive tuition usually depend in the first instance on whether their school is included in the scheme. The proportion of children taught in an LEA is usually related to the number of schools covered, but this is not always true because some authorities concentrate their resources on a few schools while others spread similar resources more thinly over a greater number of schools. Generally speaking, the secondary sector is better served than the primary sector: the vast majority of LEAs put instrumental provision into all or most of their secondary and some of their primary schools. Authorities with the widest coverage tend to be the smaller ones. Schools least likely to be included in the scheme are infant and first schools and small rural schools, and special schools which received no input from the service in nearly two-thirds of LEAs.

While many authorities have a deliberate policy of priority for, say, reaching all secondary schools or expanding provision in primary schools, a substantial number continue to distribute the service according to tradition: schools with good provision tend to attract more and those with none either find it difficult to acquire a share or simply do not try. The inequitable distribution of the service was a cause of concern in some authorities where it was felt that without an increase in resources little could be done to redress the balance.

In considering schools for instrumental tuition certain factors are usually taken into account, such as whether the school is supportive of music generally, can be reached easily by peripatetic staff, has sufficient intending players to be economically viable and can provide suitable facilities for tuition. Once a school is included in the scheme, some form of selection is used to determine which children should receive tuition since resources are not usually sufficient for everyone to try. Selection is carried out by the instrumental service or by the school or, more commonly, as a joint decision between the two. How children are selected depends very much on the people doing the selection, but certain considerations are widely believed to be important. Enthusiasm and commitment, evidence of musical ability and physical suitability are considered important almost everywhere. Parental support and evidence of musical potential are also held to be major considerations. Academic ability is much less likely to be taken into account. The age at which children can begin tuition on certain instruments is related to size and physical suitability. Most stringed instruments, however, can be scaled down in size, thus increasing opportunities for younger children to learn to play them.

No method of selection is foolproof and inevitably some children will give up, usually when the novelty has worn off, when the work becomes technically more difficult, or on transfer to another school. Other critical points occur during adolescence, especially when examinations loom. Teachers are well aware of these and other pressures on their pupils and usually encourage them to continue as far as possible. Teachers were found to hold different attitudes, however, towards children who were not progressing well. Some believed that if children were enjoying the experience they should be allowed to continue whereas others felt that scarce resources should be concentrated on those who worked hard and made progress.

A third of LEAs kept records of instrumental pupils' progress and a half made written reports to parents. Apart from their obvious functions, records and reports were considered to help give instrumental music the status of other school subjects. Most LEAs encouraged pupils to take external examinations such as those set by the Associated Board of the Royal Schools of Music and roughly one in three had devised their own local system of graded instrumental tests. Almost all LEAs made some kind of special provision for exceptionally talented children, usually in the form of financial assistance for extra specialist tuition.

All authorities provided formal group activities such as ensembles, bands, orchestras and, to a lesser extent, choirs. In many cases these groups formed a structured system through which pupils progressed. The more advanced groups usually gave performances outside their own authority and many of them toured abroad, thus providing a valuable cultural asset on a national and international scale.

6 The Instrumental Service in the School

This chapter examines the relationship between the instrumental music service and the school, and discusses how schools make provision for instrumental lessons in terms of accommodation and facilities, instruments and equipment, timetabling and practising arrangements. Observed instrumental lessons are described with regard to their aims, method and content, and the widely advocated practice of group teaching is discussed. The chapter goes on to describe links between the service and the schools, focusing on the involvement of school staff in instrumental music and peripatetic staff in school activities. Finally, the instrumental teacher's role is explored in relation to classroom music, taking account of the different perspectives of the staff concerned and the particular implications of the GCSE for potentially changing the nature of instrumental tuition in schools. The chapter draws extensively on information gathered by observation and interview in the case-study authorities.

The schools' view of the instrumental music service

School staff in the case-study authorities saw instrumental music as being very much part of the life of the school and they stressed the importance of integrating rather than isolating the work done by the service in their school. To this end, instrumental pupils were encouraged to play to their peers in assembly and perform in school concerts. In this way instrumental music was seen to be a shared rather than a selfish activity and might also inspire other children to try. One head of music expressly made the point that if instrumental tuition were removed from the schools to the music centres it would be perceived as isolated and elitist. Some schools were fortunate enough to have members of staff who could teach certain musical instruments, notably recorders or guitar and occasionally orchestral instruments. Pupils of these teachers often performed alongside children receiving tuition from peripatetic staff, thus reinforcing the notion that music provided by the school and the instrumental service was a joint enterprise. However, it is important to bear in mind that this kind of integration rests largely on the goodwill and cooperation of the staff concerned. Occasional instances were encountered where schools were unable to involve instrumental pupils in this way because their teachers lacked confidence and were reluctant to cooperate.

Instrumental music was not only believed to enrich the life of the school but was valued, particularly by headteachers, for the way in which it could enhance the school's public image. Pupils were encouraged to perform in school concerts, playing to parents and the community at large. The approval gained in this way from school governors, local councillors, the director of education and other influential individuals, was highly prized and could lead to further support and perhaps better resources. Music teachers warned, however, that this should not become the schools' overriding concern; rather they should aim primarily to communicate a love of music and develop the musical ability of their pupils.

The status of instrumental music in a school was closely related to the status of music in the school curriculum. Some headteachers reported that music was 'very much enjoyed' in their school and that their pupils were 'orientated' towards it. Orientation was attempted in several ways. For example, it was the expressed aim of some primary heads that every child should have had the opportunity to play some kind of musical instrument by the time they left the school. To help achieve this, one head had organized a three-day project in which every child in the school (infant and junior) made and played a simple instrument, participating on the last day in a performance of their own joint composition. This head described herself as a non-musician who, lacking a music specialist, aimed to make music more alive in her school. Other 'non-musician' heads were also striving to raise the status of music in their schools by attending courses and taking instrumental lessons themselves. To overcome a feeling of being 'threatened' by music, one head had successfully completed the local authority graded tests taken by her pupils. Others were participating in group tuition, taking lessons from the peripatetic teachers visiting their school. One such head, having completed Grade Three on the saxophone, regularly played in assembly in an attempt to foster a more positive attitude among his secondary boy pupils. Other strategies for highlighting music included the presenting of awards (such as Examination Grade Certificates) in assembly and the organizing of school competitions for their own 'Musician of the Year'. One middle school head was particularly pleased that his 'star' instrumental pupil was also a keen footballer because this contributed to what he described as a 'rounder image of the child'.

Besides enhancing the status of music in the eyes of their pupils, headteachers also found it necessary to try to improve music's standing with parents. Parents were said to be concerned that their children should concentrate on what they considered to be the more 'academic' subjects, and were inclined to hold music in low esteem, especially as an examination subject. Falling rolls had enabled one head to convert an empty classroom into an 'arts centre' for his pupils, but in spite of this and attempts to explain that the arts were an important part of the curriculum, parents persisted in regarding music as 'an extra'.

It was necessary in some schools to try to justify the place of music in the curriculum to teachers of other subjects. As one middle school headteacher explained, in his school instrumental music was 'the only area of the curriculum to be pursued on an individual and exclusive basis in order to achieve expertise' and this made for an uneasy truce between the instrumental service and those of his teachers who would have liked a similar specialist input in their own subjects. On the other hand, the status of instrumental music was considered by some to have improved dramatically with the advent of music centres which had transformed the image of instrumental tuition from something 'casual and cosy' into an activity which demanded high standards of per-severance and commitment.

The demanding nature of instrumental tuition was perceived by schools as having spin-off benefits for the child in that it encouraged self-discipline and increased self-confidence. Another advantage was that it gave children 'a chance to shine'. In particular, the introduction of brass into primary schools was seen to offer younger pupils the possibility of success from an early stage. While some saw this possibility as being within the reach of all children, including the academically less able, others stressed the advantages of stretching the more able, especially those with musical talent. Some teachers also said that instrumental music gave older children something to move on to when they became 'bored with singing' and provided them with 'an interest for life'.

School staff perceived instrumental music to be particularly beneficial as a social activity. First, it provided children with the shared enjoyment of taking part in group-work and ensembles. Secondly, by performing in public the music was shared with others, thus offering parents and the wider community an opportunity to be involved with children's education. The spirit of sharing was also fostered at a local level where, for example, parents with cars ensured lifts to the music centres for children without transport.

There was a striking contrast among the case-study authorities in schools' attitudes towards the providers of the instrumental music service. In two of the four LEAs views were mainly very positive and headteachers advanced such statements as: 'This authority is wonderful for music', 'We are very lucky here – the instrumental staff are absolutely dedicated', and 'The service is excellent – it provides all the instrumental music I need in my school'. Heads such as these had had good experiences of the service and, while some might have wished for more input, they were generally pleased with what they had been offered and had accepted gladly. They had also experienced an increase in provision in recent years which they attributed variously to the efforts of a new music adviser and a better organized service. In the third authority, which was less well-resourced, heads expressed a more cautious optimism.

In the fourth LEA, school attitudes to the service were inclined to be negative. All the schools involved in the project reported inadequate provision, most of them having suffered actual decreases in recent years. The problem was to some extent historical because the boundary reorganization of 1974 created a patchiness of provision which is still evident today. This contributed to discontent among heads of music who felt that the authority should ensure that 'the cake is properly shared out'. In some areas there had been an expansion of the service into primary schools but this only served to exacerbate the problem when children transferred into secondary schools which had had their provision reduced. A further difficulty in this LEA was its policy of asking parents for a 'voluntary contribution' for their child's instrumental tuition. As a matter of principle some schools refused either to collect contributions or to employ private teachers, especially in the more depressed areas. Many teachers considered that the service should be provided free, and supported the view of parents who wanted instrumental tuition for their child but did not want to pay for it *and* buy an instrument. The general feeling among the schools was that the instrumental music service was a scarce resource in their authority and lacked the specialists even to meet demands for tuition in traditional orchestral instruments, let alone the increasingly popular appeal of percussion and guitar.

The schools' relationship with instrumental staff

According to the HMI Document *Music from 5 to 16* (GB. DES, 1985d) 'much of the success of instrumental work depends upon an active partnership being maintained between schools and members of the instrumental service' (p. 21). School-based staff in our study expressed the view that peripatetic instrumental teachers should be made to feel part of the school team. They were seen as a valuable support group which extended the work done in the classroom and provided 'balance' in a very practical way. It was also pointed out that the support of school staff was vital for the success of the service in the school. Support was forthcoming when school-based teachers cooperated in arrangements made for the visits of instrumental staff; precious time could be wasted otherwise.

Coordinating this support was usually the task of the head of the music department in the secondary school or the music specialist, if there was one, in the primary school. Several primary headteachers paid tribute to the efforts of their music specialists in maintaining good relationships with the instrumental service. Where there was no music specialist, coordination usually devolved on the headteacher. In any case, it is important to remember that cooperation depends ultimately on the individuals concerned and there was therefore much variation between schools in this respect.

Music from 5 to 16 (*ibid.*) goes on to suggest that there should be at least one teacher specifically designated to liaise with all visiting instrumental teachers. Most of the schools in our study recognized the need to attempt some kind of liaison, though the extent of it varied. Usually the teacher with responsibility for music in the school undertook to organize the timetable for instrumental lessons and to make sure children attended them. In addition, some took charge of the practical arrangements for tuition and practice, chased up absentees, sorted out discipline problems and occasionally looked in on lessons. Most of them, however, experienced difficulties in actually meeting and talking with peripatetic staff. They believed that they should welcome instrumental teachers and make a point of seeing them at every visit. This was not possible if they were always teaching when the instrumental staff were in the school. Opportunities to meet over coffee in the staffroom failed to materialize if instrumental staff were teaching during break and lunch times, or if they felt unable to enter the staffroom. Some school-based staff would have welcomed more time for discussions with peripatetic teachers about children's progress, but acknowledged that this was impossible if instrumental staff had to rush away to keep appointments in other schools. They suggested that time should be allowed in peripatetic schedules for staff discussion.

Some heads and music post-holders admitted that they had little contact with their peripatetic staff who 'passed like ships in the night'. It was noticeable that theirs were the schools where there was little communication in either direction, resulting in wasted time on both sides. In one such school, pupils failed to turn up for instrumental tuition because it clashed with field trips or because events like the school sports day had been switched at the last minute, and the school complained that peripatetic staff took time off to act as examiners or give instrumental performances elsewhere.

From the instrumental teachers' point of view, experiences varied according to the school: in some they felt very much a part of the school and in others they felt surplus to it. There was a widespread feeling among peripatetic staff that instrumental music did not fit in with school music unless there were deliberate attempts to make it do so. Also, while agreeing that instrumental pupils should use their skills in school, tutors were cautious about letting children perform when they were not there to supervise their playing.

The degree of isolation experienced by peripatetic teachers depended partly on their relationship with the school and partly on timetabling. Some regarded it as their own responsibility to make contact with school staff at every visit. This could be particularly difficult to achieve in primary schools where there was no music specialist and little interest in music among the staff. It could also be a problem in secondary schools where the music block was separate from the main building, and in split-site schools. Contact also depended very much on the time of day when the school was visited: however willing the staff, liaison was virtually impossible if the visit was brief and fully taken up with instrumental teaching, especially if it occurred before normal school hours, during assembly, at break times or in the lunch hour. There would therefore seem to be a case not only for designating a member of staff to be responsible for liaising but also for extending the length of the instrumental teacher's visit to allow sufficient time for adequate liaison to take place.

Liaison between schools and instrumental staff was most likely to occur over matters such as the selection of pupils for tuition and the reporting of progress to parents (both described in detail in Chapter 5, pp. 62–74, and 74–82). It might also occur to a limited extent over the transfer of pupils from primary to secondary schools. However, in the case-study authorities transfer was mainly the responsibility of music centre personnel (see Chapter 7, pp. 108–41) or other senior staff who tried to ensure continuity of instrumental teacher where possible. The schools had little active involvement in the continuity process except in particular cases where heads of department in secondary schools visited feeder primary schools to establish relationships with pupils before transfer.

School provision for instrumental tuition

Accommodation

Accommodation for instrumental lessons varied considerably from school to school. Peripatetic teachers in the study agreed that conditions generally had improved but were often far from satisfactory. Most of them could recall lessons taught in cupboards and toilets or in cloakrooms between the rows of coats, and referred to colleagues who were still teaching under such conditions.

In primary schools the allocation of a room to music was rare and instrumental lessons usually took place in the hall, dining room, library, medical room or staff room. Some teachers had to use whichever room was available at the time and this could create acoustic problems for beginner pupils because the sound of their instruments varied in the different rooms. It could also constrain the size of the group and therefore the number of pupils which could be taught. Occasionally a spare classroom was available and teachers considered this to be the best accommodation, especially if it was situated away from the other main teaching areas. Some instrumental teachers preferred to use a piano in their lessons and this restricted them to the larger areas of the school with associated problems of noise and interruptions. Teachers generally felt that conditions were better in primary rather than secondary schools because there was likely to be more space, although this of course varied with the school. Least popular were the music blocks in secondary schools because they usually lacked adequate sound-proofing which presented problems when the adjoining practice rooms were in constant use. Practice rooms tended to be small and were sometimes too cramped for strings players, for example, to exercise the correct bowing techniques.

Instruments and equipment

Whilst the availability of pianos and audio equipment for use in instrumental lessons varied from school to school, music stands were almost always provided. Arrangements for the use of instruments and music depended largely on the authority's policy and provision. Three out of four of the case-study LEAs expected children to buy their own books and sheet music. Each authority, however, operated a different policy on instruments. The first had a generous basic stock in each school which could be supplemented by less common instruments on request from the music centre. All instruments were loaned free for an indefinite period, and both the schools and the LEA took responsibility for maintenance and repairs. The second authority also loaned instruments free for an unspecified time, but stocks in some schools were too small to meet demand. This resulted in pupils sharing an instrument which inevitably led to some dropping out unless they were willing to change to a less popular instrument. In other schools instruments stood idle because the relevant staff were not available to teach them. This problem was experienced in the third authority where stocks were retained rigidly within each school and could not be transferred for use elsewhere. While some headteachers in this LEA encouraged their parents' associations to buy instruments for the school, others objected to this practice on the grounds that parents should buy their own child an instrument as soon as possible, thereby reducing pressure on limited school supplies. In the fourth authority schools provided a limited stock for beginners only, encouraging parents to hire or purchase instruments from commercial suppliers.

Timetabling for instrumental lessons

The timing of instrumental lessons was problematic in many schools because pupils had to be withdrawn from their normal classes in order to receive tuition. At primary level this was easier because of the more integrated and flexible nature of the curriculum. Provided that the peripatetic teacher liaised with the school to avoid clashing with special activities and events such as swimming and sports day, staff were found to be generally cooperative and supportive. They rarely protested at children having to miss certain classroom activities provided that the pupils concerned made up any work missed. This was not too difficult because children of this age often worked on an individual basis and at their own pace.

At secondary level, withdrawing children from lessons required great tact and diplomacy. The secondary timetable was usually divided into subject periods taught by different teachers, and some school staff were not happy to have pupils miss all or even part of their lesson.

Some schools had a clear set of procedures whereby pupils formally informed in advance the teacher whose lesson they would be missing, requesting permission to absent themselves provided they made up their work. This system was widely adopted but with varying degrees of success. Much depended on the curricular emphasis in the school and on the attitudes of staff towards instrumental music. In 'academically-oriented' schools music was not always perceived as a worthy contestant for curriculum time and, even where the head was supportive, some teachers either forbade pupils to leave their lesson or made life so unpleasant for them that they discontinued their tuition. In an attempt to avoid disrupting lessons such as maths and English, instrumental tuition sometimes clashed with the more practical subjects, like art and home economics, where it could be especially difficult for pupils to interrupt the activity in hand. The problem increased in the upper secondary schools, particularly those which appeared to be dominated by the examination system, and instrumental staff either suspended their visits for a while, or taught the older pupils before other lessons began and during breaks and lunch hours. At least one school had arranged that fourth- and fifth-year pupils should receive their tuition at the music centre out of school hours.

Where the peripatetic teacher was in the school for several hours, it was possible to 'rotate' instrumental pupils' tuition time week by week so that they did not miss the same subject each time. The system of rotation could not be used if the peripatetic teacher's visit was short or coincided with double periods on the timetable. It was also found to be unsatisfactory because children became confused about the times of their instrumental tuition, a fact which was further complicated if the music lesson was of a different length from other school lessons. A solution, described by peripatetic and school staff as 'a blessing', seemed to lie in the seven-day cycle on which some schools operated their timetable. A seven-day timetable meant that instrumental lessons could take place at the same time each week without affecting the same lesson more than once every seven weeks and, since instrumental tuition was at a fixed time, pupils were less likely to forget to attend.

Practice arrangements

Arrangements for instrumental pupils to practise in school were piecemeal and varied from the non-existent to the highly organized. At primary level, the availability of space and supervision were important considerations and the emphasis was on encouraging children to practise daily at home. Recognizing that this was not always possible, some schools allowed children to practise during breaks and lunch hours provided there was someone to keep an eye on them. A few headteachers, who lacked a music specialist in their school, felt so strongly that once-a-week lessons were not sufficient to ensure progress that they made special arrangements for pupils to practise under supervision. With no other rooms to spare, one primary head made her office available for this purpose every day.

Secondary schools were more likely to have both a music specialist and practice rooms, and most of them allowed children to practise in their free time if they wished. A few departmental heads organized practice timetables either for individuals or groups. Children usually enjoyed playing in friendship groups and this was considered to be an excellent aid to progress. In areas affected by teacher action, however, supervised practice had been discontinued.

The instrumental lesson in school

Variation in provision

Although some instrumental tuition takes place in music centres, by far the majority of instrumental lessons take place in the schools during normal school hours. However, the amount of tuition time available varies considerably among schools receiving an input from the service. Evidence of this variation was seen in the four case-study authorities where influences such as local policy and resources, historical tradition, and factors affecting selection and take-up (discussed in Chapter 5, pp. 62–73) combined to produce an uneven distribution of provision among the cross-section of schools participating in the study. Generally speaking, the primary schools received an input of around two to three hours' instrumental teaching time per week from one or two peripatetic tutors in strings, woodwind and/or brass. The secondary schools, however, received widely differing amounts of instrumental teaching time ranging from 1½–30 hours weekly with up to seven tutors in the main orchestral groups. (Outstanding exceptions occurred in one LEA where selected schools were participating in music curriculum projects with greatly increased investment.) These findings are compatible with the survey conducted by the Assistant Masters and Mistresses Association (AMMA, 1984) which found that primary schools in the scheme were usually visited by one or two instrumental teachers and secondary schools by four or more per week.

Lesson aims

The instrumental teachers taking part in our study shared the view that they should aim to foster a love of music for its own sake rather than as a means of producing professional musicians. They wanted to communicate their own enthusiasm by involving children in new experiences through the medium of sound. They considered that, instead of simply teaching music, they were broadening children's education through music. As one tutor explained: 'I want my pupils to respond to the music, not to the dots on the page.' The emphasis was on enjoyment and they wanted lessons to be fun so that children took away something to remember and make use of later in life. The fun, however, was not without substance. In order to enjoy their playing, pupils needed to work hard so that they could feel they were making progress and producing satisfying sounds. Strings teachers in particular stressed the importance of improving difficult skills and techniques in order to derive pleasure from playing an instrument.

Enjoyment was also to be found in the social aspect of playing in groups and ensembles. The corporate nature of this kind of music-making was believed to have positive benefits for the players not only in terms of the social awareness it engendered but also in providing opportunities for the participants to perform alongside their peers and to feel they had a special contribution to make to the group.

Teaching in groups

The survey found that instrumental music pupils were taught predominantly in groups (Table 6.1).

Table 6.1: *Group and individual instrumental music teaching (94 LEAs)*

Mode of grouping	% LEAs
Pupils taught *mostly* in groups	81
Pupils taught *mostly* individually	17
Pupils taught equally in groups and individually	2
	100

Group rather than individual tuition prevailed for the majority of children in 81 per cent of LEAs. Generally this was true for pupils of both primary and secondary age, though it is important to remember that, while lessons in schools were largely on a group basis, individual tuition was often available in music centres (see Chapter 7, pp. 108–141). Although group tuition was widespread, the size of the groups tended to become smaller as children progressed. Many authorities recommended a *maximum* size of groups for the most commonly taught instruments and the recommended size was usually smaller for pupils of secondary age (Table 6.2).

Table 6.2: *Recommended maximum size of instrumental music groups (73 LEAs)*

Instrumental group	Primary pupils		Secondary pupils	
	Average	Range	Average	Range
Strings	5.8	3–15*	4.1	2–12
Brass	4.7	2–10	4.1	2–8
Woodwind	4.6	2–10	4.1	2–10

* Occasionally whole classes were taught.

The largest teaching groups were likely to be for primary violin pupils, although the recommended maximum was usually lower for strings other than the violin. At secondary level strings, brass and woodwind groups tended to be of similar size. Exceptionally large groups were usually related to specific teaching methods such as the Suzuki violin or American Band method which were adopted in a minority of LEAs, or to the innovatory groupwork of pioneers like Sheila Nelson. Teaching groups were likely to diminish as ability increased and it was not uncommon for children above the level of Grade 5 to receive individual tuition. It was also likely that pupils learning instruments which required more specialist tuition would be taught individually or at most in pairs. In addition, there were sometimes logistical reasons for teaching certain instruments to no more than one or two children at a time.

Instrumental teachers had their own views on the relative merits of group and individual tuition and often taught in accordance with their own beliefs rather than the recommendations of the authority. All four of the case-study LEAs recommended that children should be taught mainly in groups. Some teachers positively enjoyed group-teaching, believing that awkward personality clashes were less likely to occur and that pupil progress was enhanced by peer pressure. Others preferred to teach only one or two children at a time, some adding that this facilitated a closer pupil–teacher relationship. Some tutors of strings and woodwind liked to begin with large groups, gradually sub-dividing the groups according to ability as they progressed. Brass teachers sometimes grouped together players of different instruments who were of similar ability. Others objected to this on the basis that they needed to be alert to individual technical difficulties and wanted to hear the quality of sound produced by each player; one brass tutor explained: 'There is no finesse when they learn in a group'. Despite LEA policy, some teachers organized pupils into the smallest groups possible, believing that larger groups were detrimental to children's progress because 'it means taking the middle line'. Others, in deference to organizational constraints, worked ostensibly with groups but coached each child individually within the group; in a few instances children learning different instruments were taught in this way.

Length of lessons

Sometimes, both the size of instrumental teaching groups and the length of lessons were regulated by LEA recommendations on the number of pupils to be taught per hour. One authority, for example, stipulated a maximum of eight primary or four secondary pupils per hour. The time could be divided at the teacher's discretion into 15, 20, 30 or 40 minute lessons according to the number of children attending each lesson, i.e. four individual secondary pupils for 15 minutes each, two groups of four primary pupils for 30 minutes each, or two primary pupils for 20 minutes and six for 40 minutes. In practice, the length of a lesson was sometimes governed by the age and ability of the pupil: young wind players, for example, were given shorter lessons because they ran out of breath and tired more quickly than older children. Most of the lessons witnessed in the study were from 20 to 40 minutes duration.

Content of lessons

In order to look more closely at instrumental music teaching, more than 70 lessons were observed in primary and secondary schools in the four case-study LEAs. The lessons consisted mainly of tuition in a range of woodwind, brass and strings, and to a lesser extent guitar, early music and non-Western instruments. Children typically worked through a series of tutor books such as *Tune a Day, Learn as You Play, Tetratunes, Technitunes* and *Take up the Clarinet, Take up the Flute,* etc. These were often supplemented by books of studies and other published pieces, according to the level of tuition. Music ranged from well-known tunes such as nursery rhymes, songs, rounds and television themes to traditional marches and dances, pop, jazz, and classical pieces. Some teachers also made considerable use of their own compositions and arrangements. This was especially true of those working with beginners, special school pupils and groups of children at slightly different stages, or teaching instruments like steel pans for which less published material was available.

The teaching methods used in these instrumental lessons depended very much on the individual teacher. While a few adopted recognized methods such as Suzuki or Rolland, it was more often the influences of such methods that were seen rather than the methods in their entire form. Depending on the teacher, groups were taught standing freely or seated on chairs in front of music stands. A typical lesson began with tuning or warming up the instrument and playing a succession of well-known tunes. As the lesson progressed, group-playing alternated with a certain amount of solo work which allowed the teacher to pinpoint and correct individual difficulties. The playing of pieces was interspersed with the practising of scales, arpeggios and chords, the introduction of new notes and the acquisition of specific skills and techniques. While some teachers taught from behind the piano, the majority tended to mingle with their pupils, playing the instrument they were teaching and giving attention to each child as well as to the group as a whole. Given that time was precious, lessons usually proceeded at an intensive and stimulating pace, terminating with instructions about practice and preparation for the following week.

Some of the schools in which these observations took place were well-organized for instrumental music and lessons were able to proceed as planned. In others the following difficulties were noted:

> lessons wasted because pupils forgot to turn up or forgot to bring their instruments from home;
> lessons wasted or groups depleted because pupils were away at camp, on field trips, at play rehearsals and so on;
> lessons cut short because pupils arrived late from other school activities;
> lessons in halls or dining-rooms subjected to noise and interruptions especially during preparation for and clearing of school dinners;
> lessons disrupted by noise from outside during school breaks and lunch hours;
> congested, cramped surroundings requiring furniture to be cleared before lessons could begin and lesson time wasted by having to move from room to room;

shortage of music stands requiring that music be propped up wherever possible with consequent disadvantages for player's stance and posture.

These observations demonstrate the need in some schools for more care and thought to be given to providing adequately for instrumental music tuition in order that maximum use might be made of this relatively scarce resource.

Involvement of school staff in instrumental music

In the case-study authorities it was not uncommon for school-based music staff to teach an instrument in their school. At primary level, heads and class teachers with a music specialism or interest were likely to teach recorder and singing and to use any expertise they might have in other instruments, especially piano and guitar. While they might use their talents during class music lessons, many also undertook to coach choirs and recorder groups in their breaks and lunch hours. A few made a point of attending peripatetic teachers' lessons wherever possible but some found this to be unproductive because their presence was inclined to distract both the teacher and the children. At secondary level, heads of music sometimes taught their specialist instrument or, more commonly, concentrated their attentions on classroom music in which they were able to include a certain amount of percussion, keyboard, recorder and choral work. Occasionally they helped the pupils of peripatetic instrumental teachers with extra practice or theory. Many music specialists who would have been willing to make more use of their instrumental expertise found that their time was fully occupied in teaching and in organizing their department.

There was a certain amount of involvement of both primary and secondary school staff in the music centres where some teachers coached and conducted instrumental groups and choirs, and it was not uncommon in some authorities for heads of music to play a major role in running music centres (see Chapter 7, pp. 108–41). On a less regular basis, some school music staff helped out by accompanying soloists who were taking instrumental examinations or by putting in an appearance at the music centre to give their pupils a sense of support and continuity. Involvement, however, was very variable and some schools appeared to have absolutely nothing to do with the music centre in their locality.

Involvement of instrumental staff in school music activities

The existence of school-based orchestras, bands, ensembles and choirs varied from school to school, some having a well-structured range of such groups and others having none at all. At the time of the study some areas had been so badly affected by teacher action that groups of this nature had been discontinued.

There was little evidence in the case-study authorities of the regular involvement of peripatetic staff in school-based instrumental groups and choirs. This was mainly due to the fact that, apart from music centre activities, peripatetic time was fully taken up with giving lessons in schools and did not allow for assisting with school music groups. A few instrumental staff conducted and rehearsed school-based groups during lunch hours or after school, but this depended very much on their availability to be in the locality and on their willingness to give up their time. Some peripatetic teachers would have been quite happy to be involved with school orchestras, bands and choirs, had their timetables permitted. Others, on the other hand, were opposed to the idea on the grounds that, in their opinion, running and rehearsing such groups were the responsibilities of the school's music specialist. Peripatetic staff were much more likely to be involved in school concerts and performances whether at primary or secondary level. Most of them expressed a willingness not only to be present at such events but also to participate in them if required. Many also visited schools with groups of their colleagues to give recitals and workshops. In fact, two-thirds of LEAs allowed some if not all of their instrumental staff time to do this (see Chapter 3, pp. 18–40).

The instrumental teacher and classroom music

The question of whether instrumental teachers should be involved with classroom music and if so, what should be the nature of their role, has been discussed increasingly in recent years as attention has been focused on educational issues such as accountability and appraisal, the national curriculum and the new General Certificate of Secondary Education (GCSE) with its emphasis in music on a more practical approach to learning.

Our survey sought information from music advisers and heads of instrumental services on what they considered the role of the instrumental teacher should be in relation to classroom music. It was widely felt that instrumental teachers should play a supportive and complementary role especially where practical music-making was concerned. With their particular skills and experience instrumental staff could offer considerable input to classroom music and be of help to both the specialist and non-specialist teacher. It was suggested that instrumental teachers should reinforce and extend the music education begun in the classroom by encouraging and developing practical music in the school. They could also act as consultants on particular aspects of practical work such as the writing of arrangements. As one adviser said: 'The instrumental teacher should be conversant with what is going on in the classroom and willing to participate, demonstrate skills and techniques, and be drawn into mainstream music.' Indeed, the notion that instrumental staff should be conversant with what was happening in the classroom was considered to be an important link between the instrumental service and the school.

It was generally held that the instrumental teacher could and should increase musical opportunities in the classroom, and that this should include giving demonstrations and recitals to the children. There was a feeling, however, that instrumental teachers could not be expected to work in classroom situations unless they were well-supported by the staff and perceived themselves to be an intrinsic part of good instrumental practice within the school. In some authorities the instrumental service was increasingly expected to provide a larger part of music education in the schools, especially in primary schools where there was a shortage of music specialists. At secondary level, it was generally considered that the instrumental teacher should work closely with the head of music in the school and that the relationship between the two would be a critical factor in any plans to involve the instrumental service in classroom music. Respondents stressed the need for partnership, cooperation and liaison and, above all, a close working relationship between school and instrumental staff. This was not always easy to establish because instrumental teachers were constrained by tight timetables and had to rush off to visit other schools – 'the flying peri syndrome', as one adviser called it. In order for such relationships to be established it was recognized that there would have to be greater allocations of time and, moreover, positive attitudes on both sides.

Peripatetic staff occasionally went into classrooms to demonstrate instruments or to collaborate with the class teacher on specific topics. Tentative plans for more involvement in some areas had been nipped in the bud by teacher action. There was very little evidence in the case-study authorities of the actual involvement of instrumental teachers in classroom music except where special projects were being tried out.

Special projects and innovations

At the time of the study, specific attempts were being made in a number of LEAs to find ways of integrating the instrumental service with classroom music. Various pilot projects were in progress across the country, of which three very different examples are outlined below.

The first example was described as 'an experiment in partnership' between the instrumental music service and the schools. The scheme, which was being tried out in a number of primary schools, was based on the belief that instrumental music staff should use their specialist expertise and experience to support the general life and work of the school. There were three stages. First, an instrumental teacher visited the school for a day for familiarization and exchange of ideas. Secondly, a four-day period during which school staff explored ways of involving the service in their work and the instrumental teacher responded to requests for assistance, using voice or instrument to support singing, playing, groupwork, radio and TV music programmes and, where appropriate, to integrate music across the curriculum. Thirdly, a plenary day when schools and instrumental staff pooled experiences and considered implications for the future.

In the second example, instrumental music was integrated into classroom music projects. One of the purposes of this scheme was 'to orient music in schools towards a more practical base'. Teams of instrumental teachers worked with classes of first and second year pupils on curriculum music projects in a selection of secondary schools. During a typical project, schools and instrumental staff collaborated to provide 'taster' courses in a multicultural range of instruments, including electric keyboards, drums, balalaika, guitar and steel pans as well as traditional orchestral instruments.

The third example demonstrates the integration of instrumental music into multi-disciplinary projects. In this particular LEA the instrumental music service was seen as a support service with the expressed aim of 'enhancing music education as an overt component of the school curriculum, through instrumental group tuition, work-shops, recitals and curriculum development projects'. For ten weeks of the year all instrumental staff were involved in curriculum work in the form of workshops and support for projects in schools. In one such project, 1,000 children from a group of schools took part in topic-based work using music, dance, drama, art and English. Instru-mental teachers were fully involved in the project which culminated in the joint presentation, performance and display of work by both staff and children.

The influence of the GCSE

Asked whether they saw the new GCSE affecting the role of instrumental staff in the secondary school, almost all (95 per cent) of the advisers and heads of service completing the questionnaire said yes, pointing out in many cases that discussions on the matter were under way in their authority. There was a general feeling that instrumental playing would have greater recognition in the schools and that the work of the peripatetic teacher would become more central to the school music curriculum. It was widely believed that instrumental staff would be more involved not only in preparing pupils for the examination but also in assessing them. The service would have a particularly relevant role to play in practical work because of the greater emphasis in the syllabus on listening, composing and performing. This could mean a closer involvement of instrumental teachers in curriculum matters and in consultation over the materials and music to be used. To achieve this there would inevitably need to be more liaison between instrumental teachers and school-based music staff, especially heads of department.

It was expected that, as the new GCSE syllabus got under way, there would be increased demand for instrumental tuition and for specialist and stylistic skills. Instrumental teachers would also become more involved with the work of the classroom. The expected increase in demand for instrumental expertise together with more classroom involvement would have implications for peripatetic timetables. It was envisaged that much greater flexibility would be needed and that instrumental staff time in schools would have to be considerably increased. There were fears that, without extra staff, GCSE work would have to be undertaken at the expense of time traditionally devoted to instrumental tuition. Classroom involvement would call for a change of emphasis in the expertise required of instrumental teachers: they would need to develop new skills in, for example, improvisation, assessment and working with large groups. These in turn would demand more flexible approaches and perhaps a greater repertoire.

Classroom involvement would also have implications for the status and training of teachers on both sides. In-service guidance would be needed for instrumental staff in developing new skills, and for school staff in setting realistic attainment targets for pupils. While a certain amount of in-service training was considered helpful there was, however, the more fundamental problem relating to the fact that a substantial number of instrumental teachers lacked a recognized teaching qualification and were therefore classed as 'instructors' (Chapter 3, pp. 18–40). If instrumental teachers are to become more involved with teaching classroom music, it may become essential for them, like their school-based colleagues, to hold qualified teacher status. At present, however, it is not easy for those who are instructors to gain such status. Secondment from an LEA on to a PGCE course is rare, but in certain circumstances it is possible for an authority to make representations to the DES for an experienced and proven instructor to be awarded qualified teacher status (see Chapter 3).

At the time of this study, instrumental teachers themselves were uncertain of the implications of the GCSE because many of them had not yet been involved in meetings and discussions on the subject. Those interviewed in the case-study authorities expressed mixed feelings about the new syllabus and its expected effects upon their work. Some considered the GCSE to be a good thing because it was more compatible with what was actually going on in schools and would remove the barriers which had existed between GCE 'O' level and CSE pupils. Others were critical of the new examination because they believed it would not sufficiently stretch more able pupils and that it would lead to a watering-down of music education generally. While they recognized the opening-up of opportunities for a wider range of ability, they also foresaw difficulties in teaching less able children and in assessing the different ability levels.

Instrumental staff disagreed as to whether the GCSE would affect their role. Many believed that it should, but that in the long run the difficulties involved would be insurmountable. Instrumental teachers felt strongly that they ought to have more involvement with the practical elements of the new syllabus and that they had an essential contribution to make to class-based music and to group and ensemble work. They expressed reservations, however, on how this involvement could be achieved. Some feared that the growing emphasis on electronic music in schools would eventually eclipse the more traditional instruments and that their pupils would miss out on attention and resources. Others accepted that by embracing classroom music a wider range of instruments could be covered, but they failed to see how this could be achieved without diluting specialist instrumental tuition.

Further obstacles to their involvement in class-based music were concerned with time and expertise. First, peripatetic teachers pointed out that their timetables simply would not allow them to take on other activities without reducing existing instrumental teaching hours. The necessary increase in staff and resources was not, in their opinion, likely to materialize and they warned that eventually it might be the primary schools who would suffer by having to lose their allocations to the secondary sector. Secondly, many instrumental teachers had not had training or experience as classroom teachers and said they were unsure of their ability to adapt to the classroom situation. There was also a widespread feeling that heads of music in the schools, while paying lip service to the idea of involvement, might resent the presence of instrumental teachers in the classroom and be anxious about their own status and expertise.

This perceived ambivalence on the part of school staff was not evident in the views expressed by heads of department in our study. Generally, they welcomed the GCSE and saw it as having positive benefits for their work with instrumental staff. The new music syllabus was described as 'very promising' and 'the most exciting thing this century'. It offered opportunities for more pupils to explore a broader music curriculum and a wider range of instruments, and assessment would be geared to evaluating what pupils actually did rather than what they could recall. Like instrumental teachers, however, some school staff expressed concern that there might be a general lowering of standards in music which would be detrimental to the high fliers.

Heads of department stressed that, in order for the GCSE to work effectively, there would have to be a substantial increase in resources. A far greater input of instrumental staff time would be needed, since most heads of music were keen to involve peripatetic teachers in both the teaching and assessment of composition and performance. School staff said they would welcome specialist knowledge and skills to 'plug gaps' in their own expertise, especially with regard to arranging, composing, and dealing with instruments in which they were not accomplished. They recognized, however, that the difficulties of timetabling peripatetic visits to coincide with class activities would be formidable, and that in the end an insufficiency of instrumental teachers and teaching hours might prevent any real change from taking place in the role of peripatetic staff in schools.

An example of an attempt to surmount some of these difficulties was observed in one of the case-study areas. Intending GCSE music candidates from three schools met together at the local sixth-form college for one morning a month. A total of 22 fourth-formers were involved in the scheme. Its purpose was to facilitate the ensemble work which would have been impossible in individual schools on account of the low numbers taking GCSE music. Talks and visits were also planned. The scheme was staffed by two instrumental teachers and the head of music from each of the three schools, thus enabling resources and expertise to be shared. It was recognized, however, that staff communication and careful planning would be critical to the success of this scheme.

Summary

In the better-resourced case-study LEAs, schools' attitudes towards the instrumental service were warm and enthusiastic, whereas in those with more sparse provision there was discontent and frustration over the inability of the service to meet their needs. Headteachers whose schools were included in the service perceived instrumental music to be very much part of school life and particularly appreciated the way in which it could enhance the school's public image. They often found it necessary, however, to justify the place of instrumental music in the curriculum both to parents who tended to value 'academic' subjects more, and to other teachers who sometimes resented the highly specialized attention it received.

For the instrumental service to work effectively, it is important that there is support for it within the school. The attitudes of the head, and of the music specialist if there is one in the school, are vital to both the status of music in the school and communication with visiting instrumental staff. Unless deliberate attempts are made, however, communication can be difficult because instrumental staff often teach at times when school staff do not and their visits are constrained by the fact that they have to move on to other schools. Timetables rarely allow for discussion between schools and visiting staff, and it is possible for an instrumental teacher, especially in schools which are large or on split sites, to pass in and out unnoticed for several weeks. There is clearly a case for taking up the suggestion made in *Music from 5 to 16* (GB. DES, 1985d) that there should be at least one teacher in the school who is specifically designated to liaise with instrumental staff and, furthermore, time should be set aside for such liaison to take place.

Facilities for instrumental lessons were found to be very variable. Primary schools often lacked a room for the purpose and music blocks in secondary schools were seldom sound-proofed. The withdrawal of pupils from other lessons in order to receive instrumental tuition was also a problem because school staff were often reluctant for children to take time out of their classes. This situation was not fully resolved by rotating the instrumental lesson, but it is worth noting that the problem did not exist in schools which worked on a seven-day cycle. When pressures increased with the approach of 16 plus examinations, some schools arranged for their older pupils to receive tuition at the music centre after school. Perhaps there is a case for this idea to be more widely adopted.

Instrumental teachers participating in the study were aiming to foster a love and enjoyment of music in their pupils rather than producing professional musicians. They taught children mostly in groups; in fact group rather than individual tuition prevailed in most authorities although groups became smaller as pupils progressed. The recommended maximum size of groups in primary schools averaged six for strings and five for brass and woodwind, compared with four for all these instrumental groups at secondary level. In practice there were wide variations, especially in strings where occasionally whole classes were taught. Some teachers, however, did not like teaching groups and coached each child in the group in turn. If group-teaching is desirable, there would seem to be scope here for in-service guidance on how to manage it effectively.

In some areas school-based staff were involved in the music centres, but on the whole their presence at instrumental lessons in school was not found to be productive for the people involved. This contradicts the suggestion in *Music from 5 to 16* that 'designated teachers may be able to observe instrumental lessons or even join the class as participants if desired'. Similarly, in the case-study LEAs there was very little involvement of peripatetic teachers in school ensemble work, although they were usually present at school concerts and often gave recitals in schools.

It is widely believed that instrumental teachers have much to offer in supporting and complementing school music and that they should be fully conversant with what is going on in the classroom. For this to happen, however, the support must be mutual and a close relationship must be established between school and instrumental staff. This in turn requires more time as well as positive attitudes on both sides. A closer involvement of the instrumental service with class-based music was envisaged in the light of the new GCSE syllabus with its emphasis on practical music-making. It was recognized that there would be more demand for specialist skills, but at the same time there were fears that, unless resources were increased, involvement with classroom music could only be undertaken at the expense of traditional instrumental tuition. Classroom involvement also has implications for the status of instrumental staff, especially instructors, and a planned programme of in-service guidance is required for both school and visiting teachers if the necessary skills and attitudes are to be developed.

7 The Instrumental Service in the Music Centre

Introduction

Music centres are often part of the administrative structure of a service and this aspect of their role is explained in Chapter 3, pp. 27–28. This chapter is concerned with exploring the role of music centres in relation to the instrumental pupil. It begins by looking at the incidence of music centres, then examines their role in terms of the activities they offer and the pupils who participate in them. Pupil attendance at the centres is discussed, together with the various factors affecting it. The chapter includes details of music centre resources and concludes with a consideration of parental and local community involvement in the centres.

Background

As outlined in Chapter 2, pp. 5–11, the majority of LEA instrumental music services were established during the 1960s and 1970s. This period also saw the burgeoning of LEA music centres which quickly assumed an important role in most instrumental services. All but four of the authorities in our survey had music centres and in many they formed the focal point of the service for both the pupils and the instrumental staff.

The Gulbenkian inquiry, *Training Musicians* (Calouste Gulbenkian Foundation, 1978), recorded approximately 200 music centres in the 40 LEAs taking part in its survey. Our survey had responses from 94 LEAs and recorded a total of 408 music centres in 1985–86. This would seem to indicate that since 1977 the number of centres has remained fairly static.

What is a music centre?

One music centre leader believed that 'a music centre should be like a family'. This is an appropriate analogy; pupils who belong to a music centre will ideally have the support and encouragement of an 'extended family' of like-minded peers and specialist instrumental staff. Through the centre they are able to join with children from other schools in making music. The music centres are more than activity centres; they are centres of learning and in addition to furthering the musical education of the instrumental pupils attending them, play an important role in their general and social education. Some authorities refer to their music centres as music schools, perhaps because they wish to stress their 'learning' aspect. However, the activities offered and the children participating in them do not appear to differ. As the more usual name is 'music centre', it was decided for the purposes of this survey to use 'music centre' as a convenient, generic term to include both music centres and music schools.

The term 'music centre' conjures up images of a purpose-built 'centre', forming the hub of musical activity within one particular area. In many instances, the reality is somewhat different. For example, buildings designated 'music centre' are often administrative centres rather than centres of musical activity, although in some LEAs, particularly those with just one centre, they can be both. Music centres are rarely contained in any one building and most are actually comprised of a group of 'sub' – or 'satellite' – centres, with each sub-centre serving a particular locality and providing opportunities for pupils to play in area ensembles. Very few music centres are in purpose-built accommodation and the majority of sub-centres are in schools. Often, schools provide the only accommodation suitable for rehearsals of large instrumental groups, bands and orchestras. Similarly, if sound-proofed rooms are not available, the next best alternative is a large building with plenty of space to spread out the various activities.

One area music centre office was in the attic of what amounted to little better than a derelict house owned by the LEA. Some tuition took place there, but the building was not heated, there were no washing facilities, and one toilet served both staff and pupils. The centre administrator described the building as 'a health and safety hazard'. By complete contrast, another LEA was shortly to be provided with a new music centre building which was to be part of a larger cultural complex and to include an electronic studio. However, the adviser who wrote: 'Our music centre work has always been hampered by ludicrous shortages of space, with no solution at the moment in sight,' probably spoke for many in a similar plight.

Music centres are more than just *buildings* where activities happen. What makes a music centre are the ensembles and other activities it offers and the children, teachers and, occasionally, parents who participate in them.

Incidence of music centres

Bearing in mind the view of music centres outlined above, it is interesting to note that although four of the 94 authorities in our survey reported having no music centres, each of them made provision for their instrumental pupils to meet together in ensembles, bands and orchestras. One of the four, a large county, had 30 area bands and orchestras which met to rehearse in local schools. Another, a small island authority, based ensemble work in each of its four primary schools and in its one secondary school. From the pupils' point of view, attending such venues is no different from attending one of a music centre's sub-centres. The activities in these LEAs were limited to ensemble-playing and rehearsals, but as described later in the chapter, it is this type of activity which forms the basis of many music centre programmes. One adviser preferred to call the music centres in her authority 'rehearsal centres', because the main activities were orchestral and band rehearsals. Although four LEAs did not have designated 'music centres', they did provide at least some of the opportunities offered by the 90 authorities with recognized centres.

Table 7.1: *Incidence of music centres in 90 LEAs in England and Wales*

LEAs	No. of LEAs	Total no. of centres	Average no. of centres per LEA	Range
English counties	34	232	7	1–30
Metropolitan districts	29	96	3	1–10
London boroughs	17	43	3	1–9
Island authorities	3	4	1	1–2
Wales	7	33	5	1–12
Overall average			4.5	
Totals	90	408		1–30

As Table 7.1 shows, these authorities recorded a total of 408 centres between them, although this figure should be considered in the light of the many sub-centres that would exist alongside the main centres; it is possible that some LEAs would not have included all their sub-centres in the figures provided. The number of music centres in each authority varied considerably, ranging from just one to thirty. Nationally, the average number of centres per LEA was between four and five, although as Table 7.1 shows, it was higher for the English and Welsh counties than for other types of authority. Given that the counties tend to cover a wider geographical area than the metropolitan districts and London boroughs, it would seem reasonable to assume that their large geographical size creates a need for a greater number of music centres. However, the rural authorities which usually cover a very wide area tended on average to have fewer music centres, as can be seen in Table 7.2.

Table 7.2: Average number of music centres in rural, urban and mixed rural/urban LEAs

LEAs	No. of LEAs	Rural	Urban	Mixed	Overall average
English counties	34	4	2	9	7
Metropolitan districts	29	n/a	3	4	3
London boroughs	17	n/a	3	n/a	3
Island authorities	3	2	n/a	1	1
Wales	7	3	n/a	5	5
Overall average		3.5	3	7	4.5

The rural LEAs are sparsely populated and as a result cannot support a large number of music centres. Similarly the urban LEAs, which are more densely populated, also have fewer centres because the catchment areas are more compact and the centres therefore more easily accessible. For example, one city music centre was attended by approximately 1,200 pupils during the year 1985–86, but in a very large rural northern county exactly the same number of pupils attended a total of nine music centres. The highest average number of centres was, in fact, for those LEAs with a mixture of rural and urban areas and, of this category, the counties formed by far the largest group. The average number of centres for the counties with a rural/urban mix was nine, twice that of the national average. The explanation would seem to be that a relatively large geographical area, coupled with more densely-populated urban 'pockets', inevitably creates a need for more music centres.

A few authorities had one or more music 'schools' in addition to their music centres. This pyramid structure was usually found as represented in Figure 7.1. Where this extra tier of provision existed,

---

Figure 7.1: *Pyramid structure of tuition*

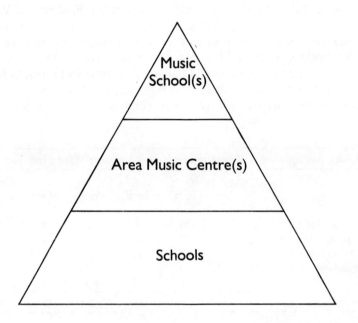

the music centres still had an 'area' centre role, serving a specific geographical area within the authority and providing opportunities to play in local ensembles. However, in these authorities, once pupils reached a certain standard they became eligible to join the 'music school'. This tended to be a county music school or the equivalent, where rehearsals of ensembles, bands and orchestras recruiting pupils from across the LEA took place. Several authorities referred to music schools as being aimed specifically at the 'talented', and most offered individual specialist tuition for their more advanced pupils. Entry was often by audition. In one authority, a School of Music had been established within each of the three music centres where 'children who have been selected from their school groups to be potentially above average instrumentalists are given a traditional and thorough instrumental, theoretical and aural training on an individual basis'. Here the term 'school' relates strongly to the concept of a more structured and academic 'learning' in the form of classes in theory, aural and general musicianship training. (See Chapter 5, pp. 79–80 for a discussion of provision for exceptionally talented children.)

Music centre activities

Pupils learning an instrument in school usually receive between 20 and 40 minutes basic group tuition a week. With individual practice this may initially meet their needs but as they progress will arguably no longer be sufficient. A varied programme of music centre activities can provide the instrumental pupil with access to specialist tuition, classes in theory, aural and general musicianship and, perhaps most importantly, the opportunity to meet with other pupils of a similar ability to play in orchestras, bands and ensembles.

Incidence of the various activities

Respondents to our questionnaire were asked to indicate which of the various activities that can take place in music centres were available to pupils attending centres in their LEA, and the results are shown in Table 7.3.

Table 7.3: *Music centre activities provided in 90 LEAs*

Activity	LEAs providing the activity	
	N	%
Ensembles, bands and orchestras	90	100
Group tuition	66	73
Individual tuition	59	66
Theory	53	59
Choirs	47	52
Aural	46	51
Musicianship	45	50
Composition/improvisation	26	29
Other activities	17	19
	(n = 90)	

The table shows clearly that all the authorities provided opportunities for pupils to play in ensembles, bands and orchestras, whereas choirs were found in only half the LEAs. Over two-thirds provided some form of instrumental tuition. Lessons in theory were given at centres in nearly 60 per cent of the LEAs, with aural work and musicianship being marginally less popular. Activities involving composition and improvisation were not so much in evidence; they occurred in under a third of the authorities.

Patterns of provision

In the majority of LEAs, the main elements of the music centre programme were ensemble-playing and some form of tuition. However, many extended this basic programme to include one or more of the following: theory, aural work, musicianship and composition/ improvisation. Nearly a quarter included all these activities. Seventeen authorities did not provide instrumental tuition in their music centres; in ten of these the centres were for ensemble-playing only, although a few also had choirs. In the remaining seven LEAs, the centres also had ensembles and choirs but, in addition, held classes in, say, theory or aural work.

Types of activity

Ensembles, bands, orchestras and choirs

The one factor common to music centres in all local authorities was that they provided ensemble-playing opportunities for instrumental pupils. This relates directly to the respondents' perception of the purpose of an instrumental service as discussed in Chapter 2, pp. 13–16: the majority felt that the service should encourage children to play together in ensembles and provide opportunities for them to do so. The fact that even those authorities without music centres provided ensemble-playing opportunities for their instrumental pupils emphasizes the importance attached to this aspect of the service.

The types of ensemble available varied from centre to centre as well as from authority to authority. Most LEAs had ensembles for all the instrument groups taught in the authority plus full-scale orchestras and bands, but this was not the case for every centre. Where pupil numbers were sufficient, music centres generally had their own orchestras and bands, but smaller centres were more likely to concentrate on smaller-scale ensemble provision. Many centres hosted rehearsals of groups recruiting on an authority-wide basis, such as a County Youth Orchestra or Band. Some centres had their own specialism; for example, one LEA had a specialist music centre for wind players.

Some LEAs were careful to provide a structured or graded system of ensembles. For example, one small London borough ran three orchestras at its Saturday morning music school: The Senior Orchestra (Grade 6 and above), The Mozart (Intermediate) Orchestra (Grades 5 and 6), and The Haydn (Junior) Orchestra (minimum standard usually Grade 3). The junior or beginners group, followed by an intermediate and then, finally, a senior group was the general pattern. Some centres structured ensembles within each instrument group in the same way. A music centre in a northern metropolitan district included in its programme preliminary, intermediate and senior string orchestras; another in the same authority ran a junior, training and senior brass band.

Fewer authorities had choirs at their music centres and from the information provided it is unclear as to whether those that did were hosting local centre-based choirs or choirs recruiting from across the authority. Nationally, about half the LEAs ran choirs at their centres; these were more common in the English counties, over two-thirds of which had choirs. Several authorities clearly expressed the view that choirs should be part of the musical life in schools and that providing the opportunity to sing in a choir was therefore the schools' responsibility.

Tuition

Despite the fact that the tuition provided by instrumental services is firmly rooted in schools, over two-thirds of authorities had group tuition in their music centres and nearly as many provided individual tuition. As Table 7.4 shows, all authorities provided some tuition in schools and in two-thirds of them most, if not all, instrumental lessons took place in schools. In none of the LEAs did lessons take place mostly in music centres.

Table 7.4: *Location of instrumental lessons in 90 LEAs*

Location	LEAs	
	N	%
Only in schools	1*	1
Mostly in schools	64	71
Mostly in music centres	0	0
Some in schools, some in music centres	25	28
	90	100

* Although respondents from ten LEAs specified that their music centres offered only ensemble-playing (see Table 7.3), nine of these indicated that *tuition* took place 'mostly in schools'. The discrepancy was explained by the fact that a few lessons, usually on specialist instruments or for more advanced pupils, did take place at their centres but as the exception rather than the rule.

In many LEAs, a wide range of instruments was taught in both schools and music centres. Overall, none of the instruments was more commonly taught in music centres than in schools and even tuition in what are considered to be the more specialist instruments such as double bass, bassoon or harp was more likely to occur in schools. However, in some authorities certain instruments were taught only in music centres. For example, of those who offered tuition on percussion, nearly a quarter did so only in music centres. The proportion was approximately the same for recorder tuition although tuition would undoubtedly be at a more advanced level than that found in schools, with pupils usually having the opportunity to learn through playing in an ensemble or consort.

It would seem, from examples of music centre timetables sent with the questionnaires, that 'group tuition' and 'ensemble playing' are often synonymous in that children learn through playing together in a group, regardless of whether they are having a lesson or rehearsing for a performance. This is particularly true for children playing in graded ensembles with other pupils of similar ability. However, in some authorities, children received ordinary group instrumental lessons in the music centre. Individual tuition was available at music centres in nearly two-thirds of the LEAs. Although sometimes offered on a second instrument, individual tuition was more commonly provided for pupils who have reached a certain level of ability and for whom a group lesson would no longer be appropriate; this was particularly so for pupils learning one of the more specialist instruments.

In school, many instrumental staff teach all or most of the instruments from one instrument group. At the music centre the same staff will teach as specialists, taking pupils to an advanced level on the instrument/s in which they specialize. Several heads of service pointed out that while the level of provision in schools 'covers most pupils for most instruments', pupils learning one of the more specialist instruments are likely, as they become more advanced, to transfer to a music centre for tuition from specialists. The area coordinator in one LEA explained that the percentage of an instrumental teacher's time spent working at a music centre is usually greater for those teaching the more specialist instruments. It can, of course, be more cost-effective to teach these instruments at the centres as specialist tuition is not always cost-effective if provided for just one or two pupils in each school.

A broader music education

One-third of the authorities provided opportunities at their centres for instrumental pupils to explore the areas of composition and improvisation. Over half the LEAs taught theory and/or aural work in their music centres and exactly half held classes in musicianship; these are subjects that cannot be covered in school time but which become increasingly important to children's musical education as their instrumental skills develop. Pupils taking Associated Board or other external examinations benefit from coaching in aural work and usually cannot progress beyond Grade 5 without passing a theory examination. In some authorities pupils were entered for external examinations through their local music centre, and in these cases, examinations were often held at the centre.

A few LEAs used their music centres for GCSE and 'A' level music tuition with pupils from a number of local secondary schools joining to form viable groups for practical sessions. One LEA ran an after-school GCSE session for those pupils experiencing timetabling difficulties in their own school.

Other activities

A number of LEAs listed other activities which extended the basic music centre diet outlined above. Some mentioned having ensembles which reflected local interests and traditions such as swing bands and handbell ringing while others had a broader range of ensembles including, for example, early music groups and jazz bands. Some centres provided activities in other performance arts. Many music centres also organized small-scale area concerts and recitals which give less advanced pupils the opportunity to gain some performance experience.

Where the music centres were an integral part of a service, their remit was often extended to include special projects and to involve younger children, parents and other adults from the local community. A typical project might be an LEA Suzuki violin class, bringing together young children and their parents to learn the violin. A few authorities held Kindermusik classes at their centres; again, these involved young children. The Kindermusik scheme, based on the work of Kodaly, Orff, Ward and Dalcroze, is designed for pre-school and infant children. It aims to develop musical literacy by working on basic aural, rhythmic and coordination skills.

Some authorities ran holiday courses for their pupils and these were mostly held at music centres. Given the normal limitations on pupil–teacher contact time, these courses afford a rare opportunity for instrumental staff and pupils to get to know each other. They enable pupils to experience working uninterrupted over a concentrated period of time ranging from one or two days to a week or more. One large London authority had a holiday music centre which ran a range of residential and non-residential courses providing about 500 of its instrumental pupils with the opportunity to play in various orchestras, bands, ensembles and vocal groups. Many LEA orchestras, bands and choirs toured both at home and abroad during the summer. In most cases the music centres were used during the holidays as rehearsal venues for these groups.

In addition to courses for pupils, some LEAs held in-service courses for their instrumental staff at the music centres. In a few cases, staff formed their own ensembles, and rehearsed and gave recitals at the centres where they were based.

Below is a list of the activities in a typical music centre programme, taken from one of six area music centres in a northern metropolitan district.

Tuition	Ensembles
Brass (lower)	Brass Ensemble
French Horn	Junior Brass Band
Trombone	Training Brass Band
	Senior Brass Band
Woodwind	Clarinet Choir
Bassoon	Woodwind Ensemble
Upper Strings	Advanced String Ensemble
Beginner Strings	Second Stage Strings
Cello	Training String Orchestra
Double bass	String Orchestra
	Training Orchestra
	Senior Orchestra
Guitar	
Piano	Junior Wind Band
Organ	Training Wind Band
	Concert Band
Theory*	Swing Band

* Although there are theory classes at this music centre, there are none in aural work and general musicianship.

This outline of music centre activities shows clearly that while the bulk of instrumental tuition takes place in schools, the centres have an important role to play in furthering that basic provision.

The music centre's role

It is difficult to discuss the role of the music centre in general because just as each instrumental service is different, so too is the role played by the music centres within a service. To some extent, role can be determined by the kinds of activities the centres offer to pupils. However, as discussed above, most authorities provide the same types of programme in their music centres. This similarity belies the variation in role both within and between LEAs. Nevertheless, it is true to say that in all 90 authorities the music centres are seen as an extension of school-based tuition; their role is to further instrumental provision in the authority by offering activities which, for a variety of reasons, may not be available to instrumental pupils in their schools.

The opportunities

All the music centres have ensembles, and many have bands and orchestras. Giving children the chance to play together in these groups is an important aspect of the role of any music centre. Ensemble-playing is not always possible in a school situation, particularly in primary schools, many of which do not have a music specialist on the staff to lead an ensemble. Even when this problem can be surmounted by the assistance of instrumental staff, the school may not have sufficient pupils of a compatible standard to form a viable ensemble.

During our study, the effects of teacher action were still being felt, and in many authorities school music had been affected quite badly. One music centre leader explained that 'on my patch, there's not one school-based orchestra or choir in any of the secondary schools'. He attributed this partly to the teachers' action but also blamed 'lack of interest' on the part of the school-based staff. However, it is perhaps important to remember that many secondary school music departments are suffering from the staffing cuts which are occurring as a result of falling rolls. Music teachers in such schools are often overworked and struggling to hold together a one-teacher department. Running bands or orchestras at lunchtimes and/or after school is not always possible, and yet this kind of activity is generally accepted as being vital to the instrumental pupil's musical development and an essential part of the learning process. In some authorities, instrumental staff are expected to help school staff with running ensembles, but one area coordinator felt this had gone too far: 'The music centres are misused,' he said, 'They should be there to supplement the work of the schools, not to do it all for them'. The adviser in the same authority thought the music centres had a crucial role to play in generating school-based activity. He felt that if music centres had their full effect and got schools working as well as they could, then the centres themselves would become redundant.

Unfortunately, many of those interviewed about their instrumental services highlighted so many problems for instrumental staff and their pupils in secondary schools in particular, that the music centres will, in some instances, almost undoubtedly remain the only place where a pupil can receive instrumental tuition. In such cases, the music centres not only extend provision in schools, they replace it.

Music centre lessons are the only option for a pupil who is keen to start learning an instrument but attends a school which does not receive the service. At secondary level, some pupils encounter problems in obtaining permission for withdrawal from their school lessons, particularly when the academic pressure of public examinations begins. One secondary school head of music had experienced 'so much hassle with withdrawal of pupils from lessons', that senior pupils' lessons were provided in the nearby music centre. One area coordinator in this LEA had recently transferred some teaching hours from secondary schools to one of his music centres for this very reason.

Sometimes it is not the attitude or internal organization of schools that affects where a pupil is taught: parents sometimes object to their children missing what they perceive as being 'proper lessons' in order to attend an instrumental lesson. Again, this concern will be most likely to arise either on the transfer from primary to secondary or from middle to upper school, or when pupils begin their GCSE courses. In such situations the music centre can provide tuition outside school time, supporting pupils with an interest in music who may otherwise have nowhere to go.

The support

This support role can extend to all instrumental pupils and may be especially important when pupils transfer from primary to secondary or from middle to upper schools. This has been identified as a particular time when some of those pupils who have been learning an instrument may decide to discontinue their lessons (see Chapter 5, pp. 74–77). It is not always possible for pupils to keep the same instrumental teacher when they transfer and the one constant factor for them could quite possibly be the music centre. If pupils are already attending a music centre, the continuity it provides may well sustain their interest when it would otherwise be lost. The supporting role is important throughout the period of learning, particularly for those pupils not receiving support at home or in school.

The social aspect

As discussed in Chapter 2, pp. 11–16, some of our respondents attached particular importance to the social aspect of learning an instrument. One centre leader hoped 'to awaken in children the pleasure that musical participation in group activity can provide'. His music centre, and others in the authority, encouraged pupils to join as soon as they were able so that they could meet other children with similar interests. The social aspect of belonging to a music centre and the other benefits this can bring would seem to be important for all pupils, but perhaps more so for those pupils who are only able to play a little and need encouragement, support, and the feeling of achievement that comes from playing with others in an ensemble. However, not all instrumental pupils have access to a music centre even when there is one in their locality. This is because some LEAs restrict access to their centres by auditioning pupils for a place, admitting only those who have reached a certain standard. The role of the music centres in these authorities is obviously quite different from that of the centres in LEAs with a policy of 'open access'.

From the documentation enclosed with the questionnaires and from the specific examples of the four case-study LEAs, it would seem fair to say that those with a more 'open access' policy see the role of the music centre in relation to pupils of all abilities and expect every child who is learning an instrument to attend their nearest centre as soon as they can play a few notes. For example, one written LEA statement said: 'children who receive free lessons in school should be expected to attend regularly as this is felt to be necessary for the development of the child's playing'. The role of the centre in such LEAs assumes increasing importance as a child develops musically and is able to participate in more activities at a higher level; at the same time, the centre is contributing to that child's development. One head of music in a secondary school explained how her area music centre had 'raised the standard of playing' by giving the pupils something to aim for through their progression up a graded system of ensembles.

The authorities with a pyramid structure also cater for all ability levels; the less advanced pupils attend the area music centres, the more advanced the LEA music school(s). When asked about the purpose of an instrumental service, many respondents felt it should aim to take all pupils to the limit of their potential. Those authorities with a pyramid structure, and the others whose centres try to cater for all ability levels, are, in theory at least, aiming for this. However, it is interesting to consider the following examples. At one extreme are LEAs in which children are auditioned, pay a fee for their place at a centre and also have to provide their own instrument. At the other extreme are those authorities which provide everything free and do not restrict access to their music centres, beyond expecting pupils to be able to play sufficient notes to render a tune. Of course, many authorities fall between these two extremes.

One large county had 30 area music centres. The principle behind the service was that children having lessons in school transferred to one of the music centres when they reached a certain standard. One instrumental teacher working in the authority explained: 'the peris are supposed to start the kids off and then get them to the music centre'. Rightly or wrongly, it was generally held that tuition at one of the area centres was superior to that in schools. The centres were staffed either by LEA instrumental teachers who were paid a sessional rate (this work was not part of their normal teaching week), or by freelance 'private' tutors. Children were not able to attend a centre until they were ten years old and should ideally have been learning an instrument for two years. However, the two centres visited during fieldwork both accepted beginners. Pupils auditioned for a place at a centre and were required to:

(i)   play or sing a short piece of music already prepared;
(ii) play or sing a short passage at sight (with assistance, where necessary); and
(iii) respond to simple aural tests to establish whether the child has a sense of rhythm and pitch.

If they passed this audition and were accepted, pupils attended the centre for instrumental tuition, aural, theory and musicianship classes and to play in an ensemble, band or orchestra. A place at the centre was only offered if the parents provided an instrument, although some centres had instruments for short-term loan. Parents also had to pay between £20 and £30 a term, according to whether their child was having group or individual tuition, with the latter being more expensive. In theory, children not paying for tuition at the local music centre could join in any of the ensembles free of charge. However, the two centres visited during fieldwork did not encourage this 'open door' policy and one centre leader explained that this was not recognized practice.

The role of the 30 area centres in this authority as 'centres of excellence' is obviously very different from those in LEAs operating an 'open access' policy, where school-based and centre-based provision are perhaps less estranged. Provision in this authority is very patchy which means that in some areas children attend music schools as beginners because there is no school-based tuition. Thus the parents of some children who want to begin lessons have no option but to pay. On the other hand, in those LEAs where the music centres cater for all abilities they are seen not only as a natural extension of school provision but also as facilitators, or as one centre leader put it, 'catalysts and coordinators for things to happen in the schools themselves'.

Pupil attendance at the music centre(s)

Eighty-three of the 90 authorities with music centres were able to provide details of the number of pupils attending their centres in the year 1985–86. It is important to bear in mind that some of the authorities gave estimates rather than exact figures.

Over 70,000 pupils attended music centres in these LEAs during 1985–86. The average attendance at any one centre was about 200, although individual centres in the urban authorities tended to cater for a larger number of pupils. The 1985–86 pupil attendance figures ranged widely from 40 in a London borough to 4,000, in an English county. If a comparison were to be made in terms of the number of schools reached by these two LEAs, they would appear to be offering the same level of provision: both reached nearly 65 per cent of their schools. However, just three per cent of those learning an instrument in the London borough attended its only music centre, whereas 42 per cent of those learning an instrument in the county attended one of 11 local music centres. The London borough had far fewer staff but in fact the ratio of FTE instrumental staff to instrumental pupils was, at 89:1, better in the London borough than it was in the county, which had a pupil–teacher ratio of 113:1.

These figures serve to highlight the differences between LEAs in the proportion of instrumental pupils attending the music centres. When the overall attendance figures are compared with the numbers of pupils learning instruments, it becomes clear that by no means all those receiving tuition attend a music centre. On average, as shown in Table 7.5, in the 70 LEAs able to provide figures for 1985–86 just over a quarter of those learning an instrument attended a local music centre.

When looking at the table it is important to remember that many of the figures provided by respondents were approximations. The table shows that in the metropolitan districts, a greater proportion of children learning an instrument in 1985–86 attended a music centre

Table 7.5: *Proportion of instrumental pupils attending music centres in 1985–6 in 70 LEAs*

Type of LEA	Proportion of pupils attending (%)				
	2–25	26–33	34–50	51–100	Average
English counties	13	7	6	1	27
Metropolitan districts	4	8	11	2	33
London boroughs	7	0	4	0	21
Island authorities	0	0	1	1	62
Wales	4	0	0	1	19
Overall average					27
Totals	28	15	22	5	

than in the counties and London boroughs. Indeed, one of the metropolitan districts had 2,000 pupils learning an instrument and, in response to the questionnaire, stated that all their instrumental pupils attended a local music centre. The Welsh counties fared less well, with just under a fifth of their instrumental pupils attending a music centre. The one exception in Wales is interesting in that the authority is much smaller than the others and more compact. Pupils there would not encounter travel problems on the scale found in some of the larger Welsh authorities where distance is obviously one factor affecting pupil attendance at the centres.

Overall, pupil attendance at music centres was surprisingly low, particularly when considered in relation to the number of pupils learning an instrument in school. If, then, only about a quarter of instrumental pupils were attending the music centres, who were they, and why were they in the minority?

Pupils attending the music centres

Sixty-nine of the 83 LEAs which gave details of pupil attendance for 1985–86 at their music centres were able to give a breakdown of the number of primary and secondary-aged children who had attended in that year. As with the general attendance figures, these numbers were, in many cases, estimates.

The Gulbenkian inquiry on *Training Musicians* (Calouste Gulbenkian Foundation, 1978) reported that of nearly 40 LEAs which responded to its 1977 survey, about one-third were catering primarily for children over the age of 11 in their music centres. In the remaining two-thirds, 'about as many children aged under 11 attended as children over 11'.

Table 7.6:   *Proportion of primary- and secondary-aged pupils attending music centres in 69 LEAs for the year 1985/6*

Pupils	LEAs	
	N	%
Primary only	1	1
Secondary only	4	6
Primary and secondary equally	9	13
More primary	19	28
More secondary	36	52
	69	100

The figures in Table 7.6 indicate that in 1985–86 the emphasis was still on provision for secondary school pupils, with the music centres in over half the LEAs being attended by more secondary-aged pupils than by those of primary age. This is hardly surprising, given that overall there are more secondary school pupils learning an instrument than primary school pupils. Only about 15 per cent of LEAs provided equally for the two age ranges; the Gulbenkian figure in 1977 was 66 per cent. This discrepancy can be accounted for by the 19 LEAs, nearly one-third, which in 1985–86 were catering predominantly for primary-aged children. The Gulbenkian report made no mention of any music centres having a primary focus in 1977 and it is possible that this development is a result of a general increase in the number of primary school children learning an instrument. This increase may also imply that some primary children are not attending their local centre because it is still geared to pupils from the secondary sector.

In one authority in our survey, the music centres were attended *only* by primary school children. In this large rural county all 31 secondary schools were visited by peripatetic instrumental staff, but primary school pupils who were learning an instrument mostly did so at the nearest music centre. Twenty-five of the 100 primary schools with pupils having instrumental lessons were visited by peripatetic staff; the majority of schools sent their pupils to the local centre. The service had a relatively small FTE of 21.5 and given the additional problem of having a large number of small schools, the solution of taking pupils to the instrumental staff is an excellent way of maximizing resources. Even so, 166 primary schools did not receive the service, chiefly because they were not within 'sensible' travelling distance of a music centre and/or because there were not enough 'travelling' staff available to visit them.

Four LEAs ran their music centres for secondary school pupils only. One of the LEAs, a large rural authority in the north of England, did not provide instrumental tuition for primary school pupils at all. In each of the four LEAs most, if not all, of the instrumental tuition took place in schools. However, one of the authorities, a northern metropolitan district, was considering moving instrumental tuition for upper school pupils out of the schools entirely and putting it into the six music centres. The head of service estimated that approximately 2,500 children were learning an instrument in his authority, but this was mainly in middle schools. He wrote that 'the upper schools perform badly' and felt that 'if GCSE fails to provide the necessary revitalization then it must be almost certain that advanced tuition will be provided entirely outside school hours at the area music centres, with a basic training service in middle schools'. There could be financial as well as logistical reasons for taking this action. LEAs are legally permitted to charge for tuition that takes place after school hours and music centre tuition usually falls into this category.

Factors affecting pupil attendance at the music centres

Pupil attendance at music centres can be limited by policies which restrict admission to children who pass an audition and perhaps, to some extent, attendance is affected in authorities where parents have to contribute financially towards the cost of centre activities. However, there are other factors which can affect pupil attendance. The location of a music centre, its times of opening and its facilities can all affect pupil attendance at a music centre, as can the attitudes of parents and of a pupil's school. In areas where there are children from certain ethnic backgrounds, cultural and religious beliefs are also factors. Not least, the interest and enthusiasm of the instrumental pupils will obviously affect their willingness to attend sessions in their leisure time, which requires greater commitment than attending a short lesson during the school day.

Pupil interest

Music centre leaders in two quite different authorities referred to the difficulty they had in persuading children to join their local music centre. One called it a 'war of attrition' but claimed that if he could somehow manage it so that a new pupil visited the centre for three weeks running, he would then have that pupil for five years or more. In this authority there were no auditions at the music centres but in the other, where auditions were necessary, the centre leader thought they were off-putting: 'A lot of children are quite happy to play their instruments in school, but are shy of going outside to play them, especially here, where they have to pass an audition first'.

One of the instrumental teachers interviewed felt it was important for her pupils to see her at the centre as it encouraged them to play in the ensembles and gave the activities status. A music centre leader saw himself as being dependent upon the teachers in primary schools to generate sufficient interest in music to motivate the pupils to join his centre, but there are many primary schools which do not have a music specialist to do this. Indeed, senior instrumental staff and advisers in several authorities expressed the view that instrumental teachers themselves should take seriously the need to engender enthusiasm in their pupils and encourage them to join the local music centre.

Perhaps there is a limit to how much instrumental teachers can achieve in what may amount to just 15 or 20 minutes contact time a week with each pupil. One adviser felt that it was up to school-based staff to interest the pupils in joining the music centre. In one authority, school-based teachers had been encouraged to accompany new pupils to the music centre. However, such collaborations are dependent upon there being a good relationship between school-based and instrumental staff, and in many cases this just does not exist. Where authorities appoint school-based teachers to work in or run the music centres, there are more opportunities for a working relationship to develop but, even then, problems can arise.

The attitudes of school-based staff

Although many music centres are actually based in secondary-school buildings, there can be tension between the music staff of secondary schools and the instrumental staff working in music centres. The most common complaint is that children experience a split allegiance when they play in both school-based and centre-based bands, orchestras and ensembles whose rehearsals and performances may often conflict. This issue concerned the Assistant Masters and Mistresses Association in its 1984 survey of music in schools. It reported, however, that it was 'clearly shown' that music centres 'do not affect the attendance in school orchestras'. It added the warning that pupils can become 'heavily committed and find it difficult giving loyalty to both centre and school'.

One music centre leader echoed this concern, but stressed that because the instrumental service was a service to *schools*, 'the school unit must come first in the pecking order' when it came to demands on a pupil's time. He also reasoned that in terms of a good relationship between schools and his centre, it was 'a bad thing to take children away from the school-based groups'.

Accessibility: the location of music centres

Not every pupil can live near a music centre and the proximity of a centre to a pupil's home is an important factor in whether or not that pupil attends.

The problems facing large authorities, particularly those that are rural, have already been touched upon. In one large Welsh county, pupils were bussed in to their nearest centre. However, they had to make their way to one of the designated 'pick-up posts' before they could catch the bus and this in itself was often difficult. One rural English county ran a pupil transport service for 'county gathering days'. The authority charged pupils 50 pence for this service which 'gathered' children who played in the county ensembles from all over the authority to enable them to rehearse together. Instrumental staff in urban areas also cited travelling distances to and from centres as one of the factors affecting pupil attendance. One leader ran a music centre which was situated in the middle of a vast council estate. He explained that it was difficult for the children to cross the estate on foot because of its layout and the distances involved, especially if they had a large instrument to carry. Many parents on the estate did not have a car and, even if they did, were often unwilling to transport their children to the centre. Pupils in urban areas may well have to travel home after dark and those with larger instruments or not living on or near a bus route often have to rely on their parents to transport them to and from the centre. Instrumental staff explained that they sometimes offered to transport pupils but they could not do this for all the children. If parents are not supportive, it is clear that there will be some pupils who, as a result, may not be able to attend their local centre. (Parental involvement in music centres is discussed below.)

When music centres open

The vast majority of music centres opened on Saturday mornings, although most opened at other times during the week as well. It can be difficult for those older pupils with Saturday jobs to participate in centre activities if these mostly take place on Saturdays. Similarly, some pupils may experience a conflict with other interests. School sports activities, for example, usually take place on a Saturday. One large authority tried to minimize this problem by opening different centres at different times; a number of centres within reasonable travelling distance each opened on a different night of the week, or on Saturday morning. Another LEA opened its centres during the evenings and on *Sundays*, thereby avoiding any potential clash with Saturday jobs. A handful of LEAs occasionally held Sunday rehearsals in their centres, usually in preparation for a specific concert.

Eighty-four LEAs had music centres opening on a Saturday morning; two of these were open all day on a Saturday. In 18 authorities, centres were open on a Saturday morning only, but by far the most popular pattern, found in 49 LEAs, was for centres to open on a Saturday morning and on one or more evenings during the week. This and other patterns of opening are shown in Table 7.7 A total of 70 LEAs opened their music centres on weekday evenings although very few (four) did so in the evenings only. Included in these figures are those whose centres were open during the 'twilight' hours, i.e. immediately after school until early evening.

Table 7.7:   *The most common patterns of term-time opening for music centres in 90 LEAs*

Time of opening	LEAs	
	N	%
Evening(s) and Saturday morning	49	55
Saturday morning only	18	20
Day(s), Evening(s), Saturday morning	15	17
Evening(s) only	4	4
All day Saturday	2	2
Evening(s) and Sunday	2	2
	90	100

Fifteen LEAs opened their centres during the day as well as at other times. One of these was the rural authority where primary school children received instrumental tuition at the music centres. Another of these authorities, also rural, had adopted the same approach. The head of instrumental tuition explained that: 'Geographical considerations weigh heavily. Much primary tuition is now centralized at selected venues and all schools in the locality are invited to send pupils for tuition'.

It would seem that in all the other authorities pupils did not attend the centres for instrumental tuition during the day. However, some LEAs held Associated Board and other external examinations at their centres and this would in some cases have entailed pupils visiting centres during the school day. In some authorities, music centres were used as a base for the instrumental staff and it is likely that their centres would be open during the day, but for administrative purposes rather than for pupil use. However, one LEA had a music centre with an electronic studio which was used regularly by the head of department from a nearby secondary school. She had very little equipment in school and had arranged access to the studio for her GCSE group. One of the authorities using a centre for GCSE and/or 'A' level tuition opened it during the day for this purpose only.

Several authorities opened their music centre doors to the local community during the day. For example, one centre housed a Senior Citizen's Orchestra every Tuesday afternoon. Twenty-one of the authorities had music centres open during the holidays, usually because they were running courses for pupils. Such courses can be of enormous benefit during the long summer holiday when it is often difficult for pupils to sustain their interest and motivation to practise.

Cultural and religious beliefs

A pupil's home and cultural background can affect his or her attendance at a centre. The problems encountered by Muslim children in particular were mentioned several times during interviews with advisers and administrative staff in multi-ethnic areas.

One music centre leader explained in detail the problems he had encountered when he first took over as centre leader; at that time, music centre activities took place on Friday evenings and Saturday mornings. There was a high proportion of Jewish children in the area and he felt it was wrong to organize music centre activities on the Jewish sabbath when many children were not allowed to attend. He spoke to local headteachers and the community rabbi and arranged for the majority of centre activities to take place on Thursday evenings instead. However, he had not foreseen the problem which would then arise from the Muslim section of the community: Thursday evening was reserved for visiting the mosque and his rescheduling of the music centre activities meant that a number of Muslim pupils in the area were no longer able to attend. The centre leader met with local Muslim community leaders who explained a further problem. It seems that while one branch of the Muslim religion is sympathetic to music and musicians, the other regards musicians with contempt. Local people holding this latter view were generally unhappy about their children attending music lessons in school and would not allow their children to learn an instrument. The centre leader had spoken further with the interested faction and was hoping to find a sub-centre located in the heart of the Muslim area of the city. He thought this would help to demystify the music centre and make it more accessible for children from Muslim families.

Establishing a music centre in the immediate locality of particular communities is an important step but there are other difficulties. For example, one instrumental teacher working in another large city commented that very often Asian girls are not allowed out alone in the evenings (an argument perhaps for Saturday morning opening), while the boys are expected to help in their parents' businesses or simply to stay at home with the family. Some children are expected to attend classes relating to their family's language or culture after school and these can place considerable demands upon them. For example, in one area, Koran classes were held two or three times a week and clashes with the centre's times of opening were inevitable.

Resources

Staffing

(a) The music centre leader
In just over three-quarters of the LEAs, each music centre had its own leader or administrator. However, for most music centre leaders, running the centre was not their main role; in fact, just nine authorities employed staff solely or primarily for this purpose. The main areas of responsibility for the majority of leaders were in other aspects of the instrumental service. Although many were ordinary instrumental teachers, a substantial number of heads of service were responsible for running a music centre and there were four LEAs in which this was part of the music adviser's brief. In 20 authorities, the music centres were run by music staff from ordinary day schools. They were usually either heads of music and other music teachers from secondary schools or, occasionally, music specialists from primary schools. In one of the case-study LEAs, the music centres were run by the heads of music in whose schools the centres were based.

The centre leader's role is an important one and in many LEAs they have a certain degree of autonomy. As outlined in Chapter 3, pp. 27–28, their job involves organizing music centre activities, ordering and checking stocks of instruments, music and other equipment and supervising the instrumental staff who work at the centre. One important aspect of their role is that of liaison, not only with parents, but also with school-based music staff. It helps if the centre leader is skilled in 'public relations' and able to sell the centre to the pupils, to the parents and to the schools. It is perhaps the centre leader more than anyone else who determines whether or not the centre is a lively place which is the focus of musical activity in the area and an integral part of the service.

(b) Instrumental staff

The music centres were, in the main, staffed by LEA instrumental teachers, who nevertheless spent the majority of their time teaching in schools. Eighty-nine LEAs gave details of music-centre staffing and all of them used their instrumental teachers in the music centres. In some authorities, teaching time in music centres was timetabled as part of an instrumental teacher's normal working week; in others, instrumental staff were paid on a sessional rate to work in the music centres. This rate usually also applied to school teachers and FE staff working in the centres.

Over a quarter of the LEAs employed 'private' tutors to teach in their centres; that is, instrumental tutors not normally employed by the authority in any other teaching capacity. In one case these would occasionally be students from the local college of higher education. A few authorities specifically mentioned that they employed professional musicians, although it is likely that some of the private tutors would also be practising musicians.

Instruments

From the literature received, it would appear that some 'main building' music centres, i.e. those acting as a base for instrumental staff and as an administrative centre for the service, are also resource centres. They house music libraries and have a stock of instruments, and several have electronic and/or recording studios.

However, while all but two authorities with music centres allocated some LEA-owned instruments to their centres, the largest proportion (34 per cent) allocated the bulk of the instruments to schools. A sizeable number allocated the instruments mainly to individual pupils (30 per cent). This would seem to make good sense as an instrument then remains with a pupil until such time as he or she no longer requires it. When instruments are allocated to schools, pupils have to change instruments when they change schools. This usually means that for the six-week period over the summer holiday, pupils who are between schools do not have access to an instrument. The time of transfer from primary to secondary schools is a 'drop out' danger zone, and not having an instrument can exacerbate the problem. Similarly, a pupil may often have to wait several weeks for the reallocation of an instrument in the new school and in extreme cases there may not be sufficient instruments in the school to meet the demand. Only two LEAs allocated their instruments mainly to the music centres. Most authorities ensured that their centres had a small stock of the most widely-taught instruments, and some stored more valuable specialist instruments there for security reasons.

Music centre income

The survey did not ask specifically about the funding or resourcing of music centres, although some LEAs included this information when answering questions about the funding of the service as a whole. In some instances, funds were allocated through the centres themselves but in most cases the centres had a small budget to cover running costs. This is discussed more fully in Chapter 3, pp. 18–40. However, the questionnaire did ask about the financial contributions made by parents towards the costs of tuition in the music centres. Although the question asked specifically for details of contributions towards tuition costs, many respondents provided details of all charges made at their music centres whether they were flat termly fees or a variety of charges for different activities, including tuition. Where parents were asked to contribute, it was more likely to be to tuition costs than to other activities. It is likely therefore that the answers to this question reflect the number of LEAs charging generally for music centre activities.

Overall, just under a third of the authorities asked parents to contribute to the cost of tuition in their music centres.

Table 7.8: *Number of LEAs in which parents contributed to tuition costs in music centres*

LEAs	Yes	No	Total
English counties	15	19	34
Metropolitan districts	4	25	29
London boroughs	6	11	17
Island authorities	2	1	3
Wales	0	7	7
	27	63	90

Table 7.8 shows that of the 27 authorities asking for parental contributions, 15 were English counties. In fact, nearly half the counties asked for parental contributions. Six London boroughs, about a third, made charges but in sharp contrast very few (four) of the metropolitan districts charged parents for their children's tuition and none of the Welsh counties did so.

There was a wide variation in the level of charges and in what they covered. Most authorities charged on a termly basis. Eight asked for a flat termly fee for membership covering all activities, including tuition where it was available. The majority had a scale of charges and parents paid according to the number and type of activities in which their children were involved.

Flat termly fees ranged between £5 and £25. One adviser explained that the fee in his authority was calculated on the basis of a parental contribution representing 50 per cent of the total annual cost of provision for their pupil, which was approximately £150. The parents' contribution was £75, which worked out at £25 a term. Another authority asked parents to contribute about 60 per cent of the total cost. A few LEAs asked for an annual registration fee, and several permitted parents' or friends' associations to collect subscriptions from parents which then helped towards various centre costs.

Thirteen LEAs had a scale of charges. They usually had one level of charges for group activities such as playing in ensembles, bands and orchestras and a higher level for tuition. One authority charged £9 a term for a 'general place' with no tuition and £15 a term for a 'special place' which included tuition. Where both group and individual tuition were offered, tuition fees were set according to which type of tuition the pupil received, and were always lower for group tuition; the difference was sometimes quite considerable. For example, one LEA charged £17 for group tuition, £24 for shared lessons and £45 for individual tuition. It was common to offer a reduction on tuition fees for a second instrument and some LEAs reduced charges for a second and third child from the same family.

In summary, nearly a third of LEAs asked parents to contribute towards costs at the music centre. Fees were usually payable termly and although a number of authorities charged a flat fee, most had a scale of charges relating to the number and type of activities in which pupils were involved. Over two-thirds of the authorities with music centres did not ask parents to contribute financially to tuition costs and this probably applied to all of the activities at their centres. Although the group charging for pupil attendance is smaller, it is significant. Charging for centre activities provides a source of much-needed income for instrumental services and as resources become scarcer it is perhaps to be expected that more LEAs will consider introducing such charges.

Charges could lead to the exclusion of some pupils from music centres on financial grounds. Some authorities included in their literature details of the circumstances under which fees could be waived. The usual criterion was that children were receiving free school meals. However, one head of service pointed out that the children who suffered were those from families just failing to qualify for benefits and he often tried to secure a waiving of fees for such pupils. In a letter to parents, one head of service regretted that the county had been forced to increase music-centre fees but wrote: 'I should like to stress that if there are financial difficulties, please do not hesitate to write in confidence to me. All requests for a reduction in fees will be carefully considered. Certainly we do not want any pupils to be prevented from learning an instrument'.

It is interesting to note that the overall attendance figures for music centres in LEAs where parents were asked to contribute financially to the costs of tuition were on average no lower and no higher than those in authorities where charges were made. However, it should not be forgotten that in those LEAs generally not making charges, i.e. the metropolitan districts and London boroughs, there are many children whose parents either genuinely could not or simply would not contribute financially in this way. Either way, their children should not be penalized; rather, the support and encouragement of their teachers and the availability of a free service become all the more important.

Parents and the community – a wider involvement

The community at large

So far, the music centres have been discussed in terms of the pupils, but some LEAs consider the involvement of the local community to be an important extension of the music centre's role. One music centre leader liked to think of his centre as 'an exchange, which is at the centre of a network, an agency for the promotion and advancement of music in the area'.

This particular centre leader gave unemployed youngsters in the area access during the day to electronic keyboards and drum kits and provided space for local rock bands to rehearse. Various music centre brochures enclosed with the questionnaire returns indicated that some LEAs made rehearsal space available to amateur groups, usually local bands and orchestras. One leader whose centre hosted a local orchestra's rehearsals felt this had a very positive effect on pupils as it gave them a chance to experience a symphony orchestra locally. It also encouraged pupils in their own playing and gave them something to which they could aspire as they progressed. This point was taken up by the head of another centre who felt that strong links between centre and community bands would benefit both sides. He cited the example of a local military band which has been in existence for over 100 years. It rehearses at the local Methodist hall and desperately needs more players. He made the point that when at the age of 18 the young people in the music centre concert band leave school and the centre, they 'drift off', having nowhere to take their playing skills and enthusiasm. This centre leader felt that if the military band were to rehearse at his centre and its members mix with the young players there, then when those players reached the age of 18 they might automatically transfer to the adult band.

Much stress is placed on ensuring continuity for pupils throughout their school career, but the transition between school and adult life is perhaps the most difficult of all. Most of those working in the instrumental service would hope that their pupils would find pleasure as adults in amateur music-making, but if links are not established between 'school' and 'community' provision, then the 'drop out' at this stage is surely inevitable.

An alternative way of establishing links would be to start a community band at the centre. However, the head of service in one of the rural Welsh counties tried to set up an adult orchestra for parents and local residents with little success: having endured severe disruption of rehearsals first during the lambing season and then at haymaking time, he eventually had to abandon the idea.

The parents

There was some evidence of a demand for adult groups at music centres, usually from parents of children attending the centres. Our questionnaire asked if parents were involved in the music centres. All but 13 of the LEAs had some level of parental involvement in their music centres, but only 11 of these officially involved parents in practical music-making. In one of the case-study authorities, one or two parents played in some of the bands and, at one centre, a father who had at first just watched his son playing in the Junior Brass Band had become the band's percussion player. His four-year-old daughter was the latest recruit: she played the triangle. Several LEAs held Suzuki violin classes for children and their parents at the music centres, and at a centre in one authority this had led to the formation of an adult string orchestra. One instrumental teacher said that he had been asked to run an adult brass band but that he had been forced to refuse because he literally had 'no hours left in the day'.

Obviously, the first priority of staff has to be to the children, and the majority of parental involvement is in centre bands intended primarily for the pupils. Few LEAs had parents receiving tuition at a centre; one centre leader said that parents often get frustrated because their progress on an instrument is so slow and noted that they tend to give up fairly quickly. Many of the instrumental staff interviewed echoed the views of the centre leader who said: 'The biggest struggle is to get the involvement of the parents'. In his area, and others like it, staff made the point that it was difficult enough to persuade parents to transport children to and from the centre, let alone to enlist their help in running it.

As discussed earlier in the chapter, lack of parental support can affect pupil attendance. Many instrumental staff on both the teaching and administrative side of the service expressed the view that pupils benefited considerably from the involvement of parents. Some were concerned that parents should take an interest in their children's activities at the local centre and support them by attending rehearsals and especially performances. Some instrumental staff thought they should have more contact with parents through, say, termly or annual parents' evenings at each area music centre.

Despite the stated problems with enlisting parental support, three quarters of the LEAs with music centres had some degree of support from parents, although case-study evidence would seem to suggest that this varies from area to area. It is generally accepted amongst music service staff that centres located in the more affluent, middle-class areas are better supported than those in more deprived areas. It is dangerous to talk of extremes, but there were, of course, examples which highlight the discrepancy between the two types of area, often within the same authority. Ironically, it is the centres in run-down inner city areas that most need the money which can be raised from the fund-raising activities of parents' groups.

Fund-raising is one of the major ways in which parents become involved with a local music centre. In the vast majority of centres their efforts were organized into 'support groups', or Friends' or Parents' Associations. One Friends' group for the music centre in a small London borough explained in a leaflet about the centre that it existed to:

(a) support the work of the centre and to encourage the musical education of the children who attend the centre

(b) encourage cooperation between parents, teachers and other agents interested in promoting and supporting the work of the centre

(c) provide financial support for all purposes relating to the work of the centre.

Fund-raising activities across the country ranged from running tuck shops and refreshment stalls at the music centres to organizing jumble sales and sponsored events. The money raised is often used to purchase instruments for the centre; these are likely to be the more expensive specialist instruments that, given current economic constraints, many LEAs cannot afford to purchase.

Support groups in some areas ran social and educational events, perhaps arranging for an outside speaker to address both pupils and parents, for example. They organized trips and concerts, helping with everything from booking a coach to designing posters and other publicity material for music centre concerts. Parents also gave help with clerical and other administrative work. Perhaps their most valued role, however, was that of transporting pupils to and from centres for classes, rehearsals and concerts. At some centres, each ensemble band and orchestra had its own support group. In one LEA, a Federation of Music Centre Parents' Support Groups had just been formed to coordinate the efforts of 14 different groups. Given this vast army of voluntary help, it was perhaps disappointing that only one respondent mentioned involving parents in policy decisions and this was 'as a sounding board' for any policy changes under consideration.

Summary and discussion

The survey found that the bulk of instrumental tuition took place in schools, but the music centres were far from being on the peripheries of the instrumental service: they emerged as having an important role to play in maximizing the potential of school-based tuition. Without exception, music centres afforded instrumental pupils the opportunity to play in ensembles, bands and orchestras alongside children of a similar ability. In addition, instrumental tuition was available at music centres in over two thirds of the 90 LEAs having such centres and many centre programmes extended to include classes in one or more of theory, aural work, musicianship and composition/improvisation.

These activities are often not available to instrumental pupils within their own schools, particularly at primary level. Similarly, the support they find at the music centre from like-minded peers and sympathetic staff is not always found in the school situation. The support role of the music centre assumes greater importance during the period of transfer from primary to secondary or between middle and upper school. The music centre can be the one constant factor, providing a degree of continuity at the time when pupils are most likely to lose interest or even discontinue lessons altogether.

The role of the music centre is to further basic provision; perhaps its most important function is the bringing together of instrumental pupils to play in ensembles, bands or orchestras. The majority of our respondents stressed that playing in ensembles was fundamental to the process of learning to play an instrument and consequently aimed to provide opportunities for their instrumental pupils to do so. However, from data provided by 70 LEAs, it would appear that during the year 1985–86, just 27 per cent of the pupils learning to play an instrument attended a music centre. Although the figures provided were, in some instances, approximations, it would be reasonable to assume that no more than a third of the instrumental pupils in those authorities were attending a music centre.

It is possible only to begin to address the question of why this is so. Pupil interest and the need for both school-based and instrumental staff to generate enthusiasm could be one factor. On a practical level, the accessibility of buildings designated 'music centre' is crucial. The majority of music centres are, in fact, local schools requisitioned for an evening or two and on Saturday mornings. It is possible that some of them could be more conveniently located, and more LEAs could follow the example of those authorities which provide transport to and from their centres. Parental attitudes and the religious and cultural beliefs of some sections of the community could also affect pupil attendance at music centres.

The survey found that music centres in over half the LEAs were attended by more pupils from the secondary than the primary sector. Although there seemed to be a trend towards providing for primary pupils, it is possible that this has not kept pace with the growing number of primary-aged pupils learning an instrument.

In LEAs where parents are asked to contribute to the cost of tuition at music centres or, indeed, where a flat fee is levied automatically, there are doubtless some pupils whose parents narrowly miss entitlement to free school meals but genuinely cannot afford to pay. It is also fair to say that where parents are asked to contribute financially, parental attitude will have far greater significance than if music centre provision were free. Finally, those centres requiring pupils to audition for places at a music centre automatically exclude some pupils from attending. The role of the music centre in an LEA which is operating an 'auditions' policy will naturally differ from that of the centre in an authority with a policy of 'open access'. In the former, children are required to reach a certain standard before they can join a music centre. In the latter, the centres *could* play an integral part in every child's musical development from the outset, enabling them to play in ensembles and to benefit from all the other activities the centres have to offer. They could but, as has been shown, in most authorities they do not.

Only a third of instrumental pupils attend a music centre, and that proportion applies equally in LEAs with an 'auditions policy' and in those authorities with a policy of open access. Two thirds of instrumental pupils are not involved in a music centre, not playing in the ensembles, not building on the basic 20–40 minute lesson a week they receive in school. If the potential of the *majority* of instrumental pupils can be maximized, and the skills engendered in their lessons fostered and developed within the context of a broader musical education, then the instrumental service will be some way on to realizing the full value of its resources. School music can and should contribute to this music education, but schools are often unable to provide the opportunities afforded by the music centres. One or two LEAs stipulate that all pupils learning an instrument must attend their local music centre. Perhaps other providers, including those with no designated music centres, should ask themselves if the instrumental pupils in their authority who do not attend a music centre are getting as much out of the instrumental service as they could.

Some LEAs have been discussing the possibility of changing the role of the music centres. A few LEAs already provide tuition for primary school pupils at the music centres because they are rural authorities and it is more cost-effective and administratively easier to do so. However, other authorities have been considering the removal of tuition from schools on financial grounds. At the time of writing this report, the Government has proposed a clause to the Education Reform Bill (GB. DES, 1987c) which will, if passed, 'permit charges for individual music tuition, taken with a parent's agreement, even when it is provided during normal school hours'.

At this stage it is only possible to speculate what the effects of this clause will be. The current position is that it is legal to charge for tuition which takes place in music centres. Some, because of this, view the location of all tuition in music centres as an alternative to making more obvious cutbacks in their service. The implications of such a move would be far-reaching. At one level, it would solve problems such as the withdrawal of pupils from 'ordinary' school lessons, but at the same time it would effectively remove instrumental tuition from the school curriculum and the school day. It would also reduce any prospect of collaboration between instrumental and school-based staff on the teaching and assessment of GCSE. Removing the service from schools altogether would leave it isolated and vulnerable. Such a move may achieve greater cost-effectiveness in the short term, but at what price?

8 Current Issues and Plans for the Future

The purpose of this chapter is to draw out the issues attracting attention in the instrumental music service at the time of the study, and to describe the plans being made by LEAs to address these issues. The discussion centres on policy and purpose, the structure and staffing of the service, budgets and charges, selection and the distribution of provision, curriculum and integration, and the role of the music centres. Questions are then raised for consideration by LEAs who are reappraising their service, and the chapter concludes with a number of recommendations aimed at improving the efficiency and effectiveness of the scheme.

Policy and purpose

In its recommendations for the instrumental service, *Music from 5 to 16* (GB. DES, 1985d) begins by saying that

> LEAs should publish their policies relating to instrumental
> work, outlining parents' and pupils' commitments, any
> financial complications, the criteria for selection, the role of the
> school and the responsibilities of the peripatetic teacher in
> relation to the school. (p.21)

The survey revealed that only one in three LEAs had a written policy for their instrumental music service, although a few more were in the process of preparing one. Most of the existing policies had been prepared by music advisers, often in consultation with senior staff in the service and in schools. They ranged in format from a few paragraphs in a teachers' information sheet to a coordinated set of booklets for teachers, parents and pupils. Statements usually related to the selection of pupils, the responsibilities of pupils and their parents, arrangements for tuition and examinations, opportunities for ensemble work, the provision and maintenance of instruments, and the recording and reporting of pupil progress.

Very few policies explicitly stated the aims of the service. One of those which did, however, based its aims on a belief in the need to provide not just for the few who may eventually become professionals but for the majority of children 'for whom the discovery of average competence will provide a lasting pleasure'. This belief was expressed in two main aims: the first to provide equal opportunities for all children able and willing to benefit from instrumental tuition, and the second to provide special facilities appropriate to the abilities thus discovered. To fulfil these aims the authority operated its service on three levels, offering opportunities for tuition and performance in schools, in music centres, and in its more specialized music schools. This service thus took the form of a pyramid, catering for a broad base of general activity and at the same time offering advanced opportunities for children with special ability.

The dilemma of whether to invest scarce resources in the talented few or to spread them more thinly among as many children as want them was evident in people's perceptions of what an instrumental service should be for. Music advisers and heads of service were divided in the priorities they accorded to these two extremes. A few, like the example given above, stated that the service should cater for both the broad base of average ability and the narrower pinnacle of special achievement. The majority, however, espoused the view that the service should be available to as many children as possible, while a substantial minority believed that it should be directed at children with a particular aptitude. The personal convictions of senior music staff, however deeply held, were not necessarily able to be put into practice. The desire to provide equal opportunities for all was often limited by severely inadequate resources. Furthermore, even where aims were expressed in policy, they did not always meet with the approval of the staff who had to carry them out, and instances were seen where teachers refused to cooperate in a policy which was at odds with their own beliefs about equity and purpose.

People's fundamental beliefs about who the service is for and what it is aiming to do will influence their views about everything to do with the role and operation of the service. The dichotomy between those who believe that instrumental tuition should be available to all who want it and those who believe it should be concentrated on pupils with special ability is likely to be reflected in opinions and, perhaps, policies on issues such as: whether the service should be free and, if not, what should be the nature of financial contributions; what staff should be recruited and how should they be deployed; whether pupils should be selected for tuition and, if so, by what criteria; the range of instruments and types of music which should be taught; and the role of the service in relation to schools.

It is important, therefore, that LEAs which have not already done so should seek to establish some consensus among both instrumental and school staff as to the main aims and purpose of their service, and agree a clear policy on how these aims might be fulfilled. At the time of the survey, one or two authorities had set up working parties with this in mind. An instrumental service with well-defined aims and a clear policy for putting them into practice is not only likely to function more efficiently but is also in a stronger position to compete effectively for much-needed resources.

Structure and staffing

The total number of full-time equivalent instrumental staff in England and Wales appears to have changed hardly at all in recent years. However, this finding must be treated with caution since it masks the severe restrictions imposed by substantial reductions in some LEAs as well as the progress made in other authorities who have increased their numbers. It must also be remembered that many of the LEAs who have maintained staffing levels consider their service to be understaffed and are unable to meet the demand for tuition in their authority. Some said that even a small increase would considerably ease the pressure on an over-stretched service, and nine LEAs were cautiously optimistic about plans to increase their staffing in the near future.

Staffing structures were found to differ enormously from one authority to another, ranging from a clear hierarchy of responsibilities in some LEAs to a single person in charge in others. To some extent structure is dictated by the size of the teaching force and by local factors such as the geographical nature of the area and the distribution of population within it. Some services, especially in the more compact urban LEAs, are administered centrally whereas others, particularly in the larger counties, are organized into separate areas each with its own staffing structure. The survey found that the widest coverage of schools tended to be achieved in smaller authorities and this may be one reason for arguing that the service in larger authorities should be divided into smaller administrative areas. Although this by itself would not increase resources, it might allow them to be deployed more efficiently.

The structure of the service has important implications not only for organization and administration but also for the career prospects of the staff. At the time of the survey, very few authorities had a clearly graded system of posts with opportunities for staff to progress. Indeed, well over half of LEAs placed all or most of their full-time instrumental teachers on the same Burnham scale. The idea of a career structure for instrumental staff was, however, beginning to take root and the government's proposals on *School Teachers' Pay and Conditions of Employment* (GB. DES, 1987a) provided an opportunity for LEAs to reappraise the situation. Twelve authorities were already making plans to reorganize and re-structure their service. Two of these were particularly concerned about staff accountability and one had set up a working party to look into matters relating to the appraisal of instrumental teachers. Before appraisal could be carried out, however, the precise nature of the instrumental teacher's job had to be clarified, and this is a task which needs to be faced in many other authorities. The survey found that only 17 per cent of LEAs provided a written job description for all their instrumental staff and, while full-timers fared better than part-timers in this respect, one in three authorities provided no job descriptions at all. The new proposals on pay and conditions (*ibid.*) raise questions for LEAs about the instrumental teacher's job. For example, to what extent should 'directed time' come under the jurisdiction of the head of service or the head of the school being visited? Should time spent at the music centre out of school hours be reckoned as part of the teacher's working week? These and many other questions will have to be resolved by LEAs before the proposals are put into effect.

The notion of a structured service with opportunities for staff development carries with it implications for in-service training. While 85 per cent of LEAs provided some form of INSET for their instrumental staff, opportunities in some authorities were very limited, occurring only occasionally. Providing INSET for a relatively small and highly specialized section of the teaching force is not without difficulties. In smaller authorities it can prove expensive unless several LEAs link together for the purpose. Supply teachers are not usually available for the release of instrumental staff, and part-time instrumental teachers may require financial inducements to attend meetings in their own time. These problems can be alleviated to some extent by providing INSET during normal teaching hours at times when tuition in schools becomes impractical, notably near the beginning and end of term.

It is important that in-service opportunities should not only be accessible to instrumental staff but that they should meet the needs of the teachers involved. Staff in some areas described INSET meetings as irrelevant and a waste of precious time. They wanted to know more about the work of their colleagues both inside and out of the LEA and abroad. Some wanted discussions on methods and techniques which would help to increase their confidence and stimulate new ideas. It was also apparent from lesson observations that some teachers needed guidance on how to teach pupils in groups, a skill which could become essential if instrumental staff are to be more involved with classroom music and the GCSE syllabus. Involvement also implies the need for instrumental teachers to be conversant with what goes on in class-based lessons. All these needs are worthy of consideration by providers of initial as well as in-service courses.

The need for a planned programme of in-service training for instrumental teachers had already attracted attention in some LEAs who were planning courses in, for example, curriculum development, assessment and support for schools. In some authorities an instrumental working group met regularly to discuss in-service requirements, a practice which could perhaps be more widely adopted, especially in view of recent changes in the funding arrangements for in-service training.

The research findings suggest that there is a need in many authorities for a more structured service: one which is not administratively unwieldy but is flexible enough to meet local needs and at the same time allows its staff a clear career structure. For teachers to work effectively and develop their professional skills, there also needs to be a clearer definition of the job they are expected to do, and a coherent programme of in-service training which is both attractive and relevant to their specific requirements. A clear staffing system with a head and a series of graded posts would not only improve morale but would enhance the status of the service, and an appropriate organizational structure would enable the service to use its resources more efficiently.

Budgets and charges

The survey found that instrumental music services in 78 per cent of LEAs had their own budget allocation, and that a further nine per cent were funded from the general music budget. The rest had no such allocation and either received a lump sum for specific purposes or relied on special requests, successful bids to general LEA funds or occasional windfalls. It is difficult to see how services which are financed haphazardly can possibly have more than a hand-to-mouth existence. A budget allocation would at least improve their status and enable them to plan for the year ahead. However, at the time of writing it is not possible to predict how the government's proposals for local financial management in the Education Reform Bill, in which schools could be responsible for managing their own budget allocations, will affect the financing of the instrumental service in each authority.

Like staffing levels, budgets from 1984–86 had remained constant in some areas and fluctuated in others: 27 per cent of LEAs, mostly counties, had increased their instrumental budget and 18 per cent, mainly metropolitan districts, had reduced theirs. Since then, further rate-capping in some areas has adversely affected music budgets: for example, in one metropolitan district the instrumental service has had to be reduced by 25 per cent.

Budgets differed in what they were expected to cover: for example, staff were often paid from central funds, and courses and travel costs were sometimes met from other special budgets. In the year 1985–86 most LEAs spent money on the repair and maintenance of instruments, but there are signs of a fall-off in spending on the purchase of instruments: 20 per cent of LEAs bought no instruments that year compared with only one per cent who had planned to buy none in 1984. With ever-rising prices, the cost of many musical instruments is prohibitive and some budgets are fully stretched in maintaining existing stocks. A growing awareness in recent years of the need to expand the range of instruments taught is not always matched by the resources with which to do it and, however willing, some LEAs are not able to provide the instruments either to meet pupil demand or to satisfy the requirements of an up-to-date curriculum.

Very few instrumental services receive sufficient LEA resourcing to meet demand, and a major dilemma facing authorities is whether to provide a free but limited service or seek some form of financial help from parents in order to increase resources and provide a wider service. The survey found that virtually all LEAs asked parents for a financial contribution of some kind whether it was towards the cost of courses, concerts and tours, external examination fees, the purchase of music, the provision of an instrument or the maintenance and repair of instruments loaned to their child. Although in a test case in 1981 it was judged illegal to charge for instrumental tuition given in school time, five LEAs had continued since then to request a 'voluntary contribution' for tuition, and 30 per cent legitimately charged for lessons at their music centres where the fee was usually subsidized by the authority to a greater or lesser extent.

Some LEAs are able to be far more generous than others and the degree of their generosity is nowhere more apparent than in the arrangements made for the provision of pupils' instruments. Authorities ranged from those who provided free loan and maintenance of LEA stocks throughout the players' school career to those who required children to supply their own from the start. The level of funding in any one authority was often attributed by senior staff to the priorities of the local council, and to the diligence of the Chief Education Officer and the music adviser in securing a share of the education budget for music. It was also widely acknowledged that, while those holding the purse-strings welcome the prestige which pupils' public performances bring to their authority, they do not always appreciate the resources which must be made available if children are to reach such a standard.

Shortly after the completion of our survey, the government put forward its proposals for a new national curriculum (GB. DES, 1987b) in which music was to be one of the foundation subjects. While this at least ensured music a place in the curriculum, there was concern in the profession for the amount of time and resources which would be left over after the priorities of the core subjects had been met. Acknowledging this, education minister Angela Rumbold told the annual conference of the National Association for Education in the Arts in October 1987 (Rumbold, 1987) that 'the amazingly high standard of many of our young performers ... is truly remarkable' and that 'we in central government will continue to do what we can to help give music in schools the encouragement it deserves'. Whether this promise will be matched in financial terms remains to be seen. At the time the promise was made, the government was inviting comments on its consultation document *Charges for School Activities* (GB. DES, 1987c) with the intention of clarifying the legal position of authorities who want to make charges. The document, which included questions about instrumental music provision, was greeted with mixed feelings. While some believe that the power to charge fees for school tuition would enable LEAs to provide a better-resourced service, others fear that children whose parents cannot afford to pay would be denied the opportunity to learn. A service which is available only to those who can afford it conflicts with principles of equal opportunity and, furthermore, runs the risk of weakening its position as an integral part of the school curriculum, since it could be perceived as an expensive option which could be removed entirely to the private sector.

At the time of writing, LEAs decide what, if any, contributions to seek from parents and the government has affirmed that, even if legislation is made, authorities will remain free to decide such matters for themselves. There is unease, however, about how such legislation might be interpreted and what pressures might be put on LEAs to raise money for services which have hitherto been provided free.

Distribution and selection

Since very few services can satisfy demand for instrumental music tuition, some form of selection inevitably occurs in terms of which schools are included in the scheme and which pupils are taught. The survey revealed considerable differences between LEAs in the proportion both of schools covered by the service and of pupils learning: school coverage ranged from 24 per cent in one authority to 100 per cent in others, while the proportion of school-age population taught ranged from two to 29 per cent. The unevenness of provision, not only between LEAs but also within them, is so great that a child's chances of learning to play a musical instrument can depend very much on where he or she lives.

The inequitable distribution of instrumental resources within LEAs was a cause of concern among advisers and, at the time of the survey, ten were planning changes in favour of more balanced provision. Uneven provision within an authority could often be traced back to local government reorganization in the seventies, and the fact that little had been done in some areas to improve this situation was attributed to a lack of resources with which to expand. However, until such expansion becomes possible, it might be worthwhile to concentrate on ways of redistributing existing resources to provide a more even service. This is no easy task because schools already receiving the service are often reluctant to take reductions so that others can benefit. One LEA with a middle-school system was proposing to tackle the problem by transferring tuition from upper schools to music centres in order to offer more provision to middle schools.

Schools which prove to be 'successful' users of the service tend to attract more provision, and this raises the question of whether resources should be concentrated upon those schools considered likely to use them best or distributed to as many schools as possible. Children attending schools with no provision are deprived of the opportunity to learn unless ways can be found of giving them lessons elsewhere, such as at the music centre or in a neighbouring school. Some LEAs, particularly those with rural areas, have solved the problem of stretching limited resources to pupils in small schools by providing opportunities for children from a cluster of schools to gather at one school or centre for instrumental tuition and other activities. This practice could perhaps be used more widely.

Providing for children with special needs, including those with exceptional musical ability, can be problematic. It is interesting to note that only 37 per cent of LEAs put instrumental tuition into their special schools compared with 88 per cent making extra provision for exceptionally talented pupils. This raises questions about which children should have priority when resources are scarce. Imbalances are often deliberate because limited resources are targetted where they are likely to yield the greatest tangible returns, namely at the pupils most likely to benefit. In this sense, 'pupils most likely to benefit' are defined in terms of musical aptitude and ability. This raises two questions. First, how can aptitude and ability be detected if children are not given the opportunity to try in the first place? Secondly, what about the 'spin-off' benefits referred to by teachers, such as increased confidence, self-discipline and 'the chance to shine'? It could be argued that these are particularly appropriate to children with special educational needs and that pupils attending special schools, instead of being near the bottom of the selection stakes, should be regarded as a priority.

The survey revealed that LEAs distribute similar amounts of resources differently: some spread theirs thinly to reach a few pupils in many schools while others concentrate theirs on more pupils in fewer schools. Input into schools covered by the scheme also varies considerably from school to school within some authorities. In general, secondary schools are likely to be offered more teaching hours on a wider range of instruments than primary schools. In recent years many LEAs have increased provision in primary schools so that children can begin learning from an earlier age. The difficulty is that it is not always possible to ensure continuity between the primary and secondary sectors, and young players are sometimes lost. Pupils may, for example, transfer to a school where there is no tuition in their instrument or where allocations are already taken up by children in the school. Gate-closing also operates if children can begin learning certain instruments only at primary age and those who did not have the opportunity at that stage are denied the chance to start at secondary school.

The selection of children to receive instrumental lessons is made by staff in the service or in the schools or, more commonly, by means of a joint decision between the two. Although certain criteria such as enthusiasm and commitment, musical ability and physical suitability are widely held to be important, the actual selection process is likely to be influenced by the attitudes of the individuals making the selection. For example, instances were found of discrimination both against and in favour of children who were considered to be less able, disruptive or disadvantaged. It would probably be helpful if LEAs published their policies on pupil selection and provided guidelines for those doing the selecting. Approximately 40 per cent of LEAs offered no such guidance.

Curriculum and integration

There is evidence that attitudes towards the instrumental music curriculum are changing and that there is now a greater range in the instruments and types of music covered by the service than hitherto. Awareness of the need to extend the range has recently been sharpened by the introduction of the GCSE syllabus with its greater scope for composing and improvising, and by the possibility it brings of a closer involvement of the instrumental service with classroom music.

The survey found that the music taught embraced a variety of periods, styles and cultures. Early instruments other than the recorder were taught in a fifth of LEAs and modern instruments such as electric guitar, keyboards and synthesizer were taught in about a third. Concert programmes indicated that a range of styles was performed including jazz and rock as well as traditional orchestral music. Special initiatives in jazz were under way in four authorities, one of which had set up a post for jazz animateur funded jointly by the LEA and the regional arts association. A small minority of LEAs had introduced tuition in non-western, mainly Indian and Afro-Caribbean, instruments.

There are signs that tuition in both modern and ethnic instruments is on the increase: seven authorities were planning to expand their range to include more guitar and electronic work, and five wanted to increase their tuition in non-Western instruments. Initiatives in electronic music were being carried out in a number of LEAs. For example, one instrumental service was developing a mobile sound technology unit for the purpose of fostering an understanding of electric music and its creative possibilities in a group of schools; another was operating a curriculum development project in the use of electronics and computers in the music classroom. Multicultural music projects were under way in eight authorities and included the appointment by one service of a development officer and four full-time teachers of Asian music.

From 1983–84 to 1985–86 there were noticeable trends in staffing for the main orchestral groups, with a marked increase in woodwind and percussion compared with a slight fall-off in strings. Initiatives in all the main groups were in progress around the country: for example, a woodwind project in conjunction with Boosey and Hawkes, primary school workshops in orchestral percussion and a pilot scheme to teach violin in first schools. The situation with regard to singing, however, was difficult to ascertain. While there had been an overall reduction in the number of singing teachers, there was a growing awareness in some authorities that choral work should be developed and, although only 27 per cent of LEAs offered voice tuition, others encouraged singing not only for its own sake but also as a foundation for all musical activity. Nonetheless, while every service provided opportunities for children to take part in orchestras, bands or ensembles, only about a half had choirs and there was a tendency in some areas to regard choral work as the responsibility of the schools rather than the service.

Schemes involving professional musicians were being planned or implemented in at least 27 LEAs. These included musicians and composers-in-residence, master classes for staff and pupils, and opportunities for children to work and perform with professional groups such as the London Sinfonietta and the Bournemouth Symphony Orchestra.

Music from 5 to 16 (GB. DES, 1985d) recommends that 'peripatetic teachers should be encouraged to provide a scheme for the school, outlining the music that is to be learnt, the stages of progress and the likely expectations'. It further recommends that 'regular written assessments of pupils' progress should be provided'. The survey showed that about a third of LEAs had some system for recording children's progress in instrumental music and a half provided written reports to parents. Record-keeping was often informal and left to the discretion of individual teachers. Although two LEAs were planning to improve their system for monitoring instrumental pupils' progress, the whole issue of accountability was one which was only just beginning to receive attention at the time of the survey. If children's instrumental work is to be accorded the same status as their other school work, there would seem to be a case for arguing that every LEA should have an appropriate system of recording and reporting instrumental pupils' progress.

Both the fieldwork in the study and the documentation provided by LEAs suggest that the actual content of instrumental lessons, and the methods by which instrumental skills are taught, are usually left to the discretion of the individual teacher. There are signs in some authorities, however, that this is beginning to change and that attempts are being made to establish some coherence with regard to both a core repertoire and a common teaching approach. Two LEAs were planning to develop schemes of work for instrumental lessons and a further five were running projects using specific methods such as Rolland and Suzuki.

A matter which was attracting more attention in the instrumental service was the need for curriculum development. At least 35 LEAs were either planning or already engaged in curriculum development initiatives, some as a result of involvement with the School Curriculum Development Committee (SCDC) 'Arts in Schools' project. Many of these initiatives were specifically related to school support and the GCSE. It was generally believed that the new GCSE syllabus would call for more integration between instrumental and school-based music staff, and it was envisaged that instrumental teachers would play a more supportive and complementary role, using their specialist skills to reinforce and develop the musical activities begun in the classroom. With a view to providing support for schools, some LEAs were planning in-service training for peripatetic staff and encouraging probationer instrumental teachers to spend more time in the classroom. A number of pilot schemes were already in operation. For example, one LEA had appointed coordinators to help primary teachers stimulate and develop a wide variety of musical activities; another had allocated each instrumental teacher to a specific school for a set period to work alongside class teachers and give group tuition, demonstrations and workshops. Such schemes are particularly appropriate in primary schools which lack a music specialist. Workshops and recitals given in schools by groups of instrumental teachers are another important element of support and several LEAs who had not already done so were planning to introduce these on a regular basis. On a much smaller scale, one or two LEAs were piloting bold projects in which instrumental and class teachers worked together to provide instrumental tuition for large groups and sometimes whole classes. One such example was the adaptation of the American Band Method to teach wind and strings to children in secondary schools, using class-based music lessons supplemented by peripatetic tuition.

The future role of instrumental teachers in relation to the GCSE was receiving considerable attention and 15 LEAs were actively engaged in preparations for involving the service in teaching the new syllabus. Preparations at that time were mainly in the form of discussion groups and the introduction of in-service courses for both school-based and instrumental teachers.

The whole notion that school and instrumental staff should work more closely together, not only for GCSE but throughout the age-range, is one which demands much consideration. There is plenty of scope for children who receive specialist tuition to use their skills more in class and school music. Much more problematic is the drawing together of the respective skills of instrumental and class music teachers. First, there has to be support within the schools, with deliberate attempts at communication and liaison between both sides. A very real difficulty is that of finding enough time for effective liaison and discussion to take place, especially in view of the new arrangements for teachers' pay and conditions. Secondly, there are fears that without more time and resources a greater involvement in classroom music can be achieved only at the expense of specialist tuition. Thirdly, some instrumental teachers are not at all sure that they have either the necessary skills or even the wish to work with whole classes or large groups.

There is a case for arguing that the music teaching staff should be viewed as a whole – all music teachers – rather than the two distinct groups of peripatetic and school-based teachers. Certainly there have been moves in this direction in initial teacher-training courses which in some institutions give the student opportunities to teach as both a class and a peripatetic teacher. While there is room for the different kinds of expertise which each group possesses, there is also a place for the particular skills and abilities of individual staff: some will be adept at working with large groups and whole classes, some will work better with individuals and small groups, and some will be able to do both. In schools there are opportunities for deploying all these skills, and ways need to be found for harnessing the competencies of both instrumental and class teachers as a team. This is perhaps the most urgent task currently facing the instrumental music service.

Music centres

The survey revealed that all but four of the LEAs taking part in the study have music centres, and that the main function of these centres is to extend the instrumental work begun in school, especially by providing opportunities for children to take part in ensembles, bands, orchestras and choirs. It appears, however, that music centres generally are under-used, since it was estimated that on average they are attended by fewer than a third of the children receiving specialist tuition.

The findings of the study suggest that there is scope for extending the role of music centres to help relieve some of the pressures and problems currently facing music teachers in schools and in the service. First, music centres often provide valuable support for the pupil and this aspect of their role could be more widely developed. The music centre could be used to ensure continuity for children who transfer to schools where tuition on their instrument is not available, and it could provide a teaching resource in areas where schools have no tuition at all. Music centres could also be more widely used during the twilight hours (from about 4pm to 7pm) to offer tuition to older pupils for whom it is undesirable to miss other school work in the day in order to attend lessons. Where it is uneconomical to send peripatetic teachers into small or remote schools, music centres might also be used more extensively as places to which children can be brought together for tuition and other musical activities. For example, one LEA has successfully piloted a scheme to reach more pupils by bringing primary children during the day and secondary children after school to centres where instrumental teachers can work with larger groups than would be practicable in individual schools.

Secondly, music centres could provide much-needed support for the teaching staff. Peripatetic teachers in particular often experience isolation, both from the staff in the schools they visit and from other instrumental staff. Some music centres function as a base for music teachers in the area, providing somewhere for them to meet for discussion, the exchange of ideas and in-service training. This function could perhaps be used more widely.

Thirdly, music centres have an important part to play in drawing the schools and the service closer together. There are fears in some areas that if tuition were removed from the schools, the instrumental service would become isolated from school music and would be perceived as an elitist enterprise which could easily be assigned to the private sector. This, however, ignores the support which the service can give to schools. Instrumental staff have two potential roles to play: that of giving specialist tuition to pupils, whether in schools or music centres; and that of providing support to schools. To be effective, this support must be two-way, the service supporting the schools and the schools supporting the service. In some areas, support from the schools extends to the involvement of school staff in the music centres; 22 per cent of LEAs have centres which are led by secondary school heads of department or primary music specialists. Music centres are also sometimes used as a resource by pupils from surrounding schools who are studying for GCSE or 'A' level music, and perhaps this practice could be more widely adopted and extended to younger children working on arts and cross-curricular projects and themes. Far from isolating the service from the schools, the music centre could thus become the hub of music activities provided by both sides.

Clearly there is scope for music teachers and pupils to work more closely together, pooling their skills and resources in both the schools and the music centres. There is also the possibility of linking their work, through the music centres, with the community at large. Ensemble work is a particularly useful means of bringing together staff, pupils and members of the public and helps to give music education a high profile. Establishing adult bands, choirs and orchestras at the music centre provides opportunities for pupils to continue with their playing after leaving school, and is worth consideration both as an important means of continuity and as an added resource for promoting music in the locality.

Conclusions and recommendations

The evidence provided by this study and described in the main chapters of this report has demonstrated the contribution which the instrumental music service makes, not only to the education of children of school age but also to cultural enrichment in this country and abroad. The study further shows that the service has a major part to play in the future of music education and that there is considerable scope for it to strengthen and widen its role. At the same time, it is abundantly clear that the service is faced with a number of issues which may be critical to its success and survival. Now, more than ever before, there is a need to take stock of existing provision and plan its development. The following questions are raised to assist LEAs in the consideration and reappraisal of their service.

- For whom is the service intended? Should the service concentrate its resources on children with special ability or, as the majority believe, should it try to find ways of giving every child who wants it the opportunity to learn to play an instrument?
- How should resources be distributed? Should they be concentrated on those schools or areas where pupils are considered most likely to benefit, or should they be spread more thinly to give access to a greater number of schools?
- How can uneven provision be made more equitable? Can ways be found of redistributing limited resources so that they can be made available to all areas of the authority?
- If the service is unable to meet demand, which children should have priority in being offered tuition? By what criteria should they be 'selected'?
- How can resources best be used to extend the range of musical styles and instruments to meet the current requirements of the music curriculum? Could more attempts be made, for example, to appoint advisory teachers and to involve professional musicians and the Regional Arts Associations in the work of the service?
- What should be the precise role of instrumental teachers with regard to the service and to the schools?
- How best can instrumental teachers be prepared to meet the needs of their pupils and of the schools they serve?
- How can the service be made more accountable, with regard to both staff appraisal and pupil progress?

These are some of the fundamental questions which need to be addressed when planning the future of the instrumental music service, and each LEA will need to consider them in relation to the particular needs and characteristics of its own area. Despite the inevitable diversity which this entails, the study has indicated that there are a number of recommendations which may be made to improve the efficiency and effectiveness of any service. The authors therefore recommend that LEAs who have not already done so should give urgent consideration to the following.

1. Each LEA should try to establish some agreement on the aims and purpose of its service and produce a written statement of its policy. This would help to put the service on a firm footing and strengthen its position when competing for scarce resources.

2. Each instrumental service should have an administrative structure with a person designated as its head; the structure must be flexible enough to meet the needs of the area; in large authorities it may be necessary to divide the service into smaller administrative areas to improve efficiency.

3. Each LEA should attempt to clarify the precise role of the instrumental teacher with regard to the service and to the schools. The LEA should provide a job description for all members of the instrumental music staff and should offer a clear career structure through which they might progress. This would not only improve staff morale and efficiency but would also enhance the status of the service.

4. Each LEA should try to ascertain the in-service needs of its instrumental music teachers. It should then provide a planned programme of in-service training which is both relevant to these needs and available at such times and places as are realistic for these teachers to attend.

5. Each LEA should consider whether it is providing an equitable service and, unless further resources are forthcoming, concentrate on ways of redistributing provision to make it more evenly accessible. Particular attention should be given to ways of increasing opportunities for children in special schools who could learn to play a musical instrument.

6. Where the service is unable to meet demand, the LEA should agree a policy and provide guidance on 'selection'.

7. Each LEA should agree a policy on the recording and reporting of pupils' progress. This would improve the accountability of the service and give instrumental music the status of other school work.

8. Each instrumental service should consider its role with regard to a closer involvement in school music. In particular, it should consider its potential role as a support for schools. If this role is to be fulfilled, the needs of schools must first be ascertained and then ways found for meeting these needs.

9. Each LEA should consider ways of drawing the instrumental service and school-based music more closely together, perhaps by viewing the staff on both sides as comprising a music team. Consideration should be given to the wider use of instrumental pupils' skills in class music, the involvement of instrumental staff in school music and the involvement of school-based staff in the instrumental service.

10. Each LEA should consider whether more use could be made of music centres to enable the service to reach more children. The role of the music centre could also be extended to provide more support for the pupil, the staff and the schools. Music centres could be more widely used as a resource for schools as well as for the service. They could also provide continuity for pupils who have left school and promote music in the community at large.

Appendix   Transfer from Old Burnham Scales to New Main Scale

Teachers other than headteachers and deputy headteachers

Transfer to main scale

2. (1) (a) Subject to paragraph 5 a teacher who was on 30th September 1987 being paid on Scale 1, 2, 2(S), 3, 3(S) or 4 or on the Senior Teacher Scale, shall on 1st October 1987 transfer to the appropriate point on the main scale set out in paragraph 6 of this Document in accordance with the following table and the notes thereto.

	Scale point on 30th September 1987						Scale point on main scale on 1st October 1987
Scale 1	Scale 2	Scale 2(S)	Scale 3	Scale 3(S)	Scale 4	Senior Teacher Scale	
0–2							1
3–4	0	0					2
5	1	1					3
6	2	2					4
7–8	3–4	3–4					5
9–10	5–6	5–6	0	0			6
11–12	7–8	7	1–2	1			7
13–14	9–10	8–9	3–4	2–3			8
15	11	10	5	4	0		9
			6	5	1		10
			7–10	6–9	2–8	0–8	11

Reproduced from the *School Teachers' Pay and Conditions Document* (GB. DES, 1987a) p.40.

References

AMMA (1984). *Music: an Endangered Subject?* London: Assistant Masters and Mistresses Association.

ATTENBOROUGH REPORT. CARNEGIE UNITED KINGDOM TRUST (1985). *Arts and Disabled People.* London: Bedford Square Press/NCVO.

BARNES, L. (1982). 'Some administrative aspects of the selection of children for instrumental music tuition in English primary schools', *Educational Management and Administration*, 10, 243–48.

BENTLEY, A. (1966). *Musical Ability in Children.* London: Harrap.

BEN-TOVIM, A. and BOYD, D. (1987). 'Music: the real thing or a waste of resources?', *Home and School*, Spring, 2, pp. 27–29.

CALOUSTE GULBENKIAN FOUNDATION (1978). *Training Musicians. A Report to the Calouste Gulbenkian Foundation on the Training of Professional Musicians..* London: Calouste Gulbenkian Foundation.

CALOUSTE GULBENKIAN FOUNDATION (1982). *The Arts in Schools.* London: Calouste Gulbenkian Foundation.

COOPER, D.J. (1985). 'Selection procedures used by peripatetic instrumental teachers', *British Journal of Music Education*, 2,1, 19–38.

ESTA (1983). The Training and Employment of String Teachers. London: The European String Teachers Association.

EVANS, C. (1985). 'Attitudes and change in instrumental teaching (Part 3)', *Music Teacher*, 16, 7, pp. 10–11.

GREAT BRITAIN. DEPARTMENT OF EDUCATION AND SCIENCE (1985a). Provision of instrumental music in primary and secondary schools. Letter sent to Chief Education Officers, January 1985.

GREAT BRITAIN. DEPARTMENT OF EDUCATION AND SCIENCE (1985b). *Better Schools.* Cmnd. 9469. London: HMSO.

GREAT BRITAIN. DEPARTMENT OF EDUCATION AND SCIENCE (1985c). *The Curriculum from 5 to 16.* London: HMSO.

GREAT BRITAIN. DEPARTMENT OF EDUCATION AND SCIENCE (1985d). *Music from 5 to 16.* London: HMSO.

GREAT BRITAIN. DEPARTMENT OF EDUCATION AND SCIENCE (1987a). *School Teachers' Pay and Conditions Document 1987.* London: HMSO.

GREAT BRITAIN. DEPARTMENT OF EDUCATION AND SCIENCE (1987b). *The National Curriculum 5 to 16. A Consultation Document.* London: HMSO.

GREAT BRITAIN. DEPARTMENT OF EDUCATION AND SCIENCE (1987c). *Charges for School Activities. Consultation Document.* London: HMSO.

IZBICKI, J. (1981). 'Piper's paymaster lament', *Daily Telegraph,* March 2nd, 1981.

MAWBEY, W.E. (1973). 'Wastage from instrumental classes in schools'. *Psychology of Music,* 1,1, pp. 33–43.

MILLS, J. (1985). 'Gifted instrumentalists: how can we recognise them?', *British Journal of Music Education,* 2,1, 39–49.

MILLS, J. (1988). *Group Tests of Musical Abilities.* Windsor: NFER-NELSON.

RUMBOLD, A. (1987). *Speech by the Minister of State at the Annual Conference of the National Association for Education in the Arts on Wed. Oct. 28th 1987* (unpublished).

SWANN REPORT. DEPARTMENT OF EDUCATION AND SCIENCE (1985). *Education for All.* London: HMSO.

TAYLOR, D. (1979). *Music Now.* Milton Keynes: Open University Press.

THOMPSON, K. (1985). *Wind Bands and Brass Bands in School and Music Centre.* Cambridge: Cambridge University Press.

TRODD, G. (1978). 'Instrumental music in British education', *Music Teacher,* 57,10, pp. 13–15.

UKCMET(1982). *Musical Giftedness in the Primary School: Guidelines for Teachers.* Knebworth: Pullen Press.

THE NFER RESEARCH LIBRARY

Titles available in the NFER Research Library

TITLE	HARDBACK *ISBN*	SOFTBACK *ISBN*
Joining Forces: a study of links between special and ordinary schools (Jowett, Hegarty, Moses)	0 7005 1179 2	0 7005 1162 8
Supporting Ordinary Schools: LEA initiatives (Moses, Hegarty, Jowett)	0 7005 1177 6	0 7005 1163 6
Developing Expertise: INSET for special educational needs (Moses and Hegarty (Eds))	0 7005 1178 4	0 7005 1164 4
Graduated Tests in Mathematics: a study of lower attaining pupils in secondary schools (Foxman, Ruddock, Thorpe)	0 7005 0867 8	0 7005 0868 6
Mathematics Coordination: a study of practice in primary and middle schools (Stow with Foxman)	0 7005 0873 2	0 7005 0874 0
A Sound Start: the schools' instrumental music service (Cleave and Dust)	0 7005 0871 6	0 7005 0872 4
Course Teams–the Way Forward in FE? (Tansley)	0 7005 0869 4	0 7005 0870 8
The LEA Adviser – a Changing Role (Stillman, Grant)	0 7005 0875 9	0 7005 0876 7

For further information contact the Customer Support Department, NFER-NELSON, Darville House, 2 Oxford Road East, Windsor, Berks SL4 1DF, England. Tel: (0753) 858961   Telex 937400 ONECOM G Ref. 24966001

KING ALFRED'S COLLEGE
LIBRARY